# Palgrave Macmillan Studies in Banking and Financial Institutions

**Series Editor**
Philip Molyneux
Sharjah University
Sharjah, UAE

The Palgrave Macmillan Studies in Banking and Financial Institutions series is international in orientation and includes studies of banking systems in particular countries or regions as well as contemporary themes such as Islamic Banking, Financial Exclusion, Mergers and Acquisitions, Risk Management, and IT in Banking. The books focus on research and practice and include up to date and innovative studies that cover issues which impact banking systems globally.

More information about this series at
http://www.springer.com/series/14678

Giusy Chesini · Elisa Giaretta
Andrea Paltrinieri
Editors

# Financial Markets, SME Financing and Emerging Economies

*Editors*
Giusy Chesini
Department of Business Administration
University of Verona
Verona, Italy

Andrea Paltrinieri
Department of Economics and Statistics
University of Udine
Udine, Italy

Elisa Giaretta
Department of Business Administration
University of Verona
Verona, Italy

Palgrave Macmillan Studies in Banking and Financial Institutions
ISBN 978-3-319-54890-6     ISBN 978-3-319-54891-3   (eBook)
DOI 10.1007/978-3-319-54891-3

Library of Congress Control Number: 2017936038

Cover credit: Rowan Romeyn/Alamy Stock Photo

Printed on acid-free paper

This Palgrave Macmillan imprint is published by Springer Nature
The registered company is Springer International Publishing AG
The registered company address is: Gewerbestrasse 11, 6330 Cham, Switzerland

# Acknowledgements

First of all, we would like to thank all the contributors, the most important resource for this edited book. We would like to thank also all the participants of the 2016 Wolpertinger Conference organized by the European Association of University Teachers of Banking and Finance in August–September 2016 for their invaluable comments about all the papers included in this volume and all the other referees. We would like to express our gratitude to Prof. Philip Molyneux (Professor of Banking and Finance and Dean of the College of Business, Law, Education and Social Sciences), Editor-in-Chief for the Palgrave Macmillan Studies in Banking and Financial Institution Series, for approving our proposal and for his support during the publication process. Finally, our thanks go to the Palgrave Macmillan team, Aimee Dibbens and Natasha Denby for their support during the process.

# Contents

# List of Figures

# List of Tables

# 1

# Introduction

## Giusy Chesini, Elisa Giaretta and Andrea Paltrinieri

This book investigates different aspects of the financial system, starting from the relationship between firms and banks to conclude with relatively new financial instruments, with a focus on emerging markets as well. In particular, the book analyses small and medium-sized enterprises (SMEs) access to credit, the earning quality and the cost of debt in the European Union. Moreover, it investigates an important risk measure in financial markets: credit default swaps (CDS), before going deep inside one of the most important emerging markets, China, to

G. Chesini (✉) · E. Giaretta
Department of Business Administration,
University of Verona, Verona, Italy
e-mail: giusy.chesini@univr.it

E. Giaretta
e-mail: elisa.giaretta@univr.it

A. Paltrinieri
Department of Economics and Statistics,
University of Udine, Udine, Italy
e-mail: andrea.paltrinieri@uniud.it

© The Author(s) 2017                                                          **1**
G. Chesini et al. (eds.), *Financial Markets, SME Financing and Emerging Economies*,
Palgrave Macmillan Studies in Banking and Financial Institutions,
DOI 10.1007/978-3-319-54891-3_1

assess monetary policy and the relationship between financial institutions and real estate firms.

These chapters were originally presented as papers at the annual conference of the European Association of University Teachers of Banking and Finance Conference (otherwise known as the Wolpertinger Conference) which was held at the University of Verona, Italy, at the beginning of September 2016.

Chapter 2, 'Access to Bank Credit: The Role of Awareness of Government Initiatives for UK SMEs', by Raffaella Calabrese, Claudia Girardone and Mingchen Sun, through the survey data on UK SMEs, investigates the relationship between bank credit availability and awareness of government initiatives. This is an important topic, due to the vital role that SMEs play in most countries, but their access to bank credit remains a key concern for both academics and practitioners. To encourage banks to extend lending to SMEs, the UK government has launched several initiatives in the aftermath of the most recent financial crisis. The authors find that: (1) SMEs aware of Funding for Lending Scheme are less likely to experience overdraft rejections; and (2) SMEs aware of the Business Growth Fund or the British Business Bank are less likely to experience loan rejections. However, our analysis reveals statistically weak associations among these variables.

Chapter 3, 'Earnings quality and the cost of debt of SMEs', by Federico Beltrame, Josanco Floreani and Alex Sclip, analyses the relationship between earnings quality and the cost of debt. The authors, based on a panel of Italian SMEs over the period 2004–2012, find a negative association between accruals quality and the cost of debt for SMEs. The results hold even when controlling for different measures of accruals quality, alternative determinants of bank debt and the potential endogeneity between leverage and earnings quality.

Chapter 4, 'Demand and supply determinants of credit availability: evidence from the current credit crisis for European SMEs', by Paola Brighi and Valeria Venturelli, examines the importance of demand and supply factors in determining credit availability during the recent financial crisis for different sample of in some principal European countries. The authors show that during crisis time, the credit demand is mainly driven by liquidity problems. As for the determinants of credit demand, it emerges a different pattern emerges among countries more bank than market oriented. Then, controlling for the supply of credit, two types of credit rationing have been investigated. Weak rationing defines the condition for which firms asking for credit at the same interest rate did not receive it. To be strongly bank dependent implies a greater probability to be weakly credit rationed in crisis times. Differently solid accounting data, collateral and greater size may loosen such a condition. Finally, the authors control for strong rationing, i.e. the condition for which a firm even if ready to accept worse interest rates is subject to rationing. Evidence suggests that relationship lending attitude as well as larger size could weaken the rationing condition; differently collateral as well as R&D propensity may exacerbate it because of moral hazard risk and higher information asymmetries.

Chapter 5, 'What is and what is not regulatory arbitrage? A review and syntheses', by Magnus Willesson, reviews 91 research articles and addresses the analytical foundations of regulatory arbitrage in the literature in a search for operative definitions, theories and methodological concerns. Regulatory arbitrage is an avoidance strategy of regulation that is exercised as a result of a regulatory inconsistency. As a regulatory response strategy, it has been in the shadow of other possible determinants of regulatory development. Despite the observation that many studies treat regulatory arbitrage as a phenomenon that everyone implicitly knows, the review shows that an explicit understanding of regulatory arbitrage and its motives remains scattered. Theoretically speaking, the chapter concludes that the dominant approach is that when a regulatory arbitrage opportunity exists, it is utilised. However, several theories examining the opportunity costs related to the use of regulatory arbitrage are also identified. Both methodologically and empirically, the chapter concludes that regulatory arbitrage as a strategic choice is characterised as a non-action of an event, thus delimiting the opportunities to conduct empirical research. Transaction-based regulatory arbitrage is more straightforward, and several studies therefore present measures of regulatory arbitrage. More precise and operative definitions and expanded eclectic theoretical understanding of drivers may spur stronger empirical research and regulatory development.

Chapter 6, 'Forecasting models and probabilistic sensitivity analysis: an application to bank's risk appetite thresholds within the Risk Appetite Framework', by Maurizio Polato, Josanco Floreani, Giuseppe Giannelli and Nicola Novielli, investigates the implications of a probabilistic forecasting model for determining risk tolerance thresholds under a RAF environment. Bank's financial planning requires forecasting models that allow to forecast and measure the effects of possible future scenarios. Both environmental changes and regulatory innovations even more stimulate, especially under stress scenarios, the development of simulation-based forecasting models specifically devoted to assess bank's financial soundness and capital adequacy, along with the persistency of equilibria. The rationale of employing sophisticated quantitative methods in bank's decision-making should be rooted in the compelling need to adequately manage uncertainty concerning the most relevant exogenous and policy variables for bank's management. The very promising implications of implementing the Risk Appetite Framework are to be traced in a rapidly changing approach to bank's management where the system of risks is a fundamental part of financial planning, rather than just being a by-product of it. Indeed, the RAF approach while becoming a fundamental tool for strategic control, allowing to represent mission and strategies by means of quantitative variables, enables the management to link risk targets to bank's operations.

Chapter 7, 'The determinants of CDS spreads: the case of banks', by Maria Mazzucca, Caterina di Tommaso and Fabio Piluso, analyses the determinants of CDS spreads of 86 international banks from 2009 to 2012 and empirically tests the explanatory power of credit risk, bank-specific, market and country-level factors. The authors find the following results: (1) the explanatory power of the model increases when bank-specific and market/country variables are considered; (2) capitalisation and size are the most relevant factors in determining the banks' CDS spreads; (3) when the rating decreases, the CDS premium increases, and this increase is significant when switching from investment to non-investment grade banks; and (4) the market volatility and slope of the yield curve affect the CDS spreads.

# 2

# Access to Bank Credit: The Role of Awareness of Government Initiatives for UK SMEs

Raffaella Calabrese, Claudia Girardone
and Mingchen Sun

## 2.1   Introduction

Small and medium-sized enterprises (SMEs) offer employment opportunities to millions of people worldwide and thus have often been described as the engines of economic growth in modern economies. In the UK, SMEs constitute 99.9% of all businesses in the private sector at the beginning of 2015. They also contribute 15.6 million jobs, 60% of all private sector employment and £1.8 trillion annual turnovers, 47% of all private sector turnovers.[1]

Typically, bank debt (overdrafts and loans) acts as one of the main external financing sources for SMEs. However, unlike large firms, SMEs are often young businesses and are potentially unable to provide sufficient collateral (Armstrong et al. 2013). SMEs are informationally opaque because of their lower external monitoring and narrow reporting needs compared to larger firms (Berger et al. 2006; Udell 2015). Therefore,

R. Calabrese · C. Girardone (✉) · M. Sun
University of Essex, Colchester, UK
e-mail: cgirard@essex.ac.uk

© The Author(s) 2017
G. Chesini et al. (eds.), *Financial Markets, SME Financing and Emerging Economies*,
Palgrave Macmillan Studies in Banking and Financial Institutions,
DOI 10.1007/978-3-319-54891-3_2

banks are more likely to consider them as risky borrowers and are generally more reluctant to extend loans to them, which makes them more likely to face credit constraints. The most recent financial crisis has resulted in an even worse situation for small businesses: Fraser's (2012) empirical study, for example, shows that UK SMEs suffered a significantly higher bank debt rejection rate and higher costs of applying for loans during 2007–2009 (the first phase of the financial crisis) compared with the earlier years 2001–2004, which were characterised by a lending boom.

In order to increase access to bank credit for SMEs, the UK government has proposed several initiatives and put them into effect in recent years. This chapter examines the role of the awareness of government initiatives to support SMEs using the survey data from the UK Small and Medium-Sized Enterprise Finance Monitor (SMEFM) database on access to finance.[2] Our analysis offers some evidence that SMEs that are aware of any of the government initiatives have lower rejection rates. Specifically, SMEs that are aware of Funding for Lending Schemes are less likely to experience overdraft rejections; and SMEs that are aware of Business Growth Fund or the British Business Bank are less likely to experience loan rejections. The study provides some pointers in what could be the potential drivers of this awareness. One possible answer could be found in the level financial literacy of the individual(s) running the small business.

The study is organised as follows: Sect. 2.2 provides a synopsis of the most common UK government initiatives and a review of key studies focusing on the effect of government initiatives in both developed and developing countries. Section 2.3 reports detailed information on the survey data and provides some description of the trends in bank debt rejection rates and awareness of government initiatives. Section 2.4 provides a discussion of the main findings. Finally, Sect. 2.5 concludes.

## 2.2    Government Initiatives

To incentivise banks to extend lending to small businesses, the UK government has implemented a variety of initiatives in the aftermath of the most recent financial crisis. These include the Enterprise

Finance Guarantee Scheme (EFGS), the British Growth Fund (BGF), the British Business Bank (BBB), the Funding for Lending Scheme (FLS) and the Start Up Loans Scheme (SLS). Section 2.2.1 presents an overview of the main features of these government schemes, while Sect. 2.2.2 reviews selected studies on the impact of government policy on lending to SMEs.

## 2.2.1   UK Government Initiatives to Support SMEs' Access to Finance

The EFGS was launched in January 2009[3] and is essentially a loan guarantee scheme that was established to back the small businesses which have been rejected because of their lack of collateral or proven track records when they apply for commercial loans. By 2013, it had already supported more than 20,000 UK SMEs. With this scheme, although the government is involved in the lending process, the right of decision-making is fully delegated to banks.

The BGF[4] was created in May 2011 to provide an independent fund of £2.5 billion as equity investment for British SMEs facing financial constraints as barriers for their future development. The fund is owned by five large banking institutions: Barclays, HSBC, Lloyds, RBS and Standard Chartered, and can be considered the largest long-term equity investment company in the UK. The BGF demands a minority equity stake and a board seat in privately owned, profitable SMEs, in return for an investment of £2–10m of growth capital.

The FLS was launched by Bank of England and HM Treasury in July 2012 and was designed to stimulate bank lending to SMEs by reducing the cost of bank finance (Bank of England 2012). It supplies funding to banks where both the price and the amount of the funding are associated with their lending performance to SMEs. Therefore, if banks can supply more credit for SMEs, they can obtain cheaper prices and larger availability of funding from the scheme.

The BBB[5] is a development bank that is 100% owned by the government but is managed independently. The initial intention, announced in September 2012 with £1 billion government funding, was to execute some specific government initiatives, including providing advice and create a "one-stop-shop" service for SMEs. Followed by additional funding injections, the bank was properly launched in November 2014. The bank does not provide lending to SMEs directly, but it works together with some other financial intermediaries (banks, leasing companies, venture capital funds and Web-based platforms) to promote SMEs' better access to bank credit, especially young and faster-growing companies.

Finally, it is worth mentioning the support for start-ups via the SLS,[6] a government scheme targeted at early-stage businesses. The scheme offers government-backed unsecured personal loans to individuals with a fixed interest rate at 6% and free support and guidance on their business plan with an assignment of delivery partners by the scheme.

This section presented a brief overview of some of the most important schemes that have been made available to UK small and medium businesses post-crisis and that are either backed up or initiated by the government. The next section offers a brief literature survey of selected studies on the impact of government initiatives on access to finance with reference to the UK as well as other developed economies in Europe, the USA and Japan; and developing countries, such as Africa and the Middle East.

## 2.2.2 Effects of Government Initiatives: A Brief Survey of the Literature

Government initiatives to support small and medium businesses have been widely proven to be beneficial to bank credit availability and local economic growth in both developed and developing economies.

Craig et al. (2005) examine the effect of Small Business Administration (SBA) loan guarantee programme in the USA. Employing loan-specific data, economic condition data and deposit data during the period 1990–2001, they perform panel regressions and find that SBA-guaranteed lending has a positive and significant impact on local and regional economic performance (measured by per capita income). A subsequent research carried out by Hancock et al. (2007) confirms the positive relationship between the SBA programme and economic performance proxied by output, employment and dollar payrolls. Estimating OLS regressions on annual state-level data for 1990–2000, they also demonstrate that "SBA-guaranteed loans are less procyclical and less affected by capital pressures on banks than non-guaranteed loans" (p. 4). In this sense, SBA programmes can be used as a tool to mitigate the negative effects of macroeconomic shocks on lending to SMEs.

Zecchini and Ventura (2009) focus on Italy's state-funded guarantee scheme (SGS) for SMEs. Using accounting data over 1999–2004, they employ fixed-effect panel estimations to evaluate the effect of SGS on bank credit availability and borrowing cost of SMEs. They also apply the difference-in-difference (DID) approach and test for time trends. The supply of bank credit is estimated to increase by 12.4% at the median, while the borrowing cost to reduce by about 16–20%. Bartoli et al. (2013) examine the effects of the funds provided by mutual guarantee institutions (MGIs) to small businesses during the peak of the financial crisis (2007–2009) in Italy. MGIs often arise from public initiative and they tend to operate at local level. In their study, the authors identify the determinants of the probability that a borrowing SME could be in financial distress and, therefore, receiving funds from MGIs. The authors find that MGIs have a key role especially in times of crisis.

Therefore, this suggests that the government initiative to support SMEs was generally proven to be effective in Italy, consistent with the findings of the effectiveness in the UK (Allinson et al. 2013, reviewed below), the USA (Craig et al. 2005; Hancock et al. 2007) and Japan (Uesugi et al. 2008). This latter study focuses on one of the most famous initiatives for SMEs in Japan, that is the so-called Special Credit Guarantee (SCG) programme. Using a panel data over 1998–2001, Uesugi et al. (2008) separate the sample into 1344 SCG users and 2144 non-users and find a higher loan extension among users, especially for the long-term loans. They also apply the two-step estimation procedure (with probit regression in the first step and OLS in the second step) and illustrate that the SCG programme leads to an increase in credit market efficiency. From a different view, Wilcox and Yasuda (2008) investigate the effect of the same programme on banks' guaranteed and non-guaranteed lending to SMEs. Employing a panel dataset including information for 145 individual city and regional banks in 1996–2002, they use the instrumental-variable (IV) estimation method and find different results for city and regional banks. Specifically, at city banks, the SCG programme contributes to increases in both guaranteed and non-guaranteed lending, implying a complementary relationship, whereas a substitution relationship is revealed at regional banks.

Using the firm-level survey data collected during January to March in 2012, Allinson et al. (2013) conduct a comprehensive investigation to evaluate the rationale for the UK Enterprise Finance Guarantee Scheme. They find that the scheme has not only fulfilled its original aims and targets to help SMEs get better access to credit, but has also been able to bring economic gains with a benefit-cost ratio of 7.1. Allowing for its viability and cost-effectiveness, the scheme is recommended to be expanded and cover more UK SMEs.

Concerning studies carried out in developing and emerging countries, Abor and Biekpe (2006) focus on some financing initiatives in Ghana which do not involve commercial finance by conventional financial institutions, such as Export Development and Investment Fund (EDIF), Business Assistance Fund (BAF) and Africa Project Development Facility (APDF). Using survey data for 124 SMEs with less than 100 employees, they provide some descriptive statistics to show the low awareness and usage of these initiatives. Besides, most initiatives are also thought to be difficult to access, because of lack of securable assets and lack of knowledge by finance providers about the nature of respondents' business.

Similarly, looking at bank credit to SMEs in the Middle East and North Africa, Rocha et al. (2011) use the data in 1996–2002 from a joint survey of the Union of Arab Banks and the World Bank, to detect the effect of partial credit guarantee (PCG) schemes. Employing OLS and two-stage least squares methods, they find a positive relationship between PCG schemes and SME bank lending. They also reveal that in the context of SMEs financing, the PCG schemes could have a key role in a weak financial infrastructure environment only if they were well-designed and cost-effective.

This brief review has shown that typically the effectiveness of government initiatives to support small and medium businesses has proved successful in the context of both developed and developing countries and that the benefits for the economy have typically largely exceeded the costs. Most existing studies, however, do not seem to consider the relationship between rejection rates and the actual *awareness* of government initiatives. This is an interesting and novel perspective because if awareness is by definition "knowledge that something exists" (Cambridge Dictionary) then it seems reasonable to assume that the first condition for such government initiatives to be successful is indeed for small businesses to be aware of these programmes, which might be related to the financial literacy of individuals–entrepreneurs running the small businesses.[7] Relative to SMEs that are unaware of government initiatives, SMEs with awareness are believed to be more competent to make some favourable adjustments, or even seek some support to get better access to bank credit. The relationship between bank rejection rates and awareness of government initiatives is covered below. But first, Sect. 2.3 offers some details on the UK SME Finance survey database that is used for the analysis.

## 2.3 The Small- and Medium-Sized Enterprise Finance Monitor (SMEFM)

The database SMEFM provides firm-level survey data that are regularly updated; we focus on the period 2011 Q1Q2 to 2015 Q2.[8] The surveys are carried out quarterly by interviewing around 5000 different SMEs in each survey (17 waves in total), with the interviewees carefully selected being representative samples of UK SMEs by size, sector and region. The database asks for their experiences of seeking and obtaining external finance in the previous 12 months, as well as the characteristics of the enterprises and their owners.

As Storey pointed out back in 1994, "there is no single, uniformly acceptable, definition of a small firm" (p. 8). The most common definition used in Europe is the definition set by the European Commission (EC): an enterprise with less than 250 employees and either no more than €50 million annual turnovers or no more than €43 million total balance sheet. However, the definition utilised in the SME Finance

Monitor database is slightly different from the EC definition. That is, an enterprise must have no more than 250 employees and no more than £25 million annual turnover, considerably lower than the limit set by the EC. Except for these two quantitative criteria, the surveyed SMEs should also have the following two characteristics to qualify for the interviews: (1) not 50%+ owned by another company; and (2) not run as a social enterprise or as a not-for-profit organisation.

## 2.3.1 Trends in the Bank Debt Rejection Rates and the Awareness of Government Initiatives

Figure 2.1 and Table 2.1 illustrate the trends in the bank debt rejection rates and in the awareness of government initiatives over the period under investigation.

Figure 2.1 focuses on the bank debt rejection rates. Following Armstrong et al. (2013), "the rejection rate is defined as the proportion of firms which applied for credit and were either refused outright or received less credit than they requested, as a proportion of firms applying" (p. R41).

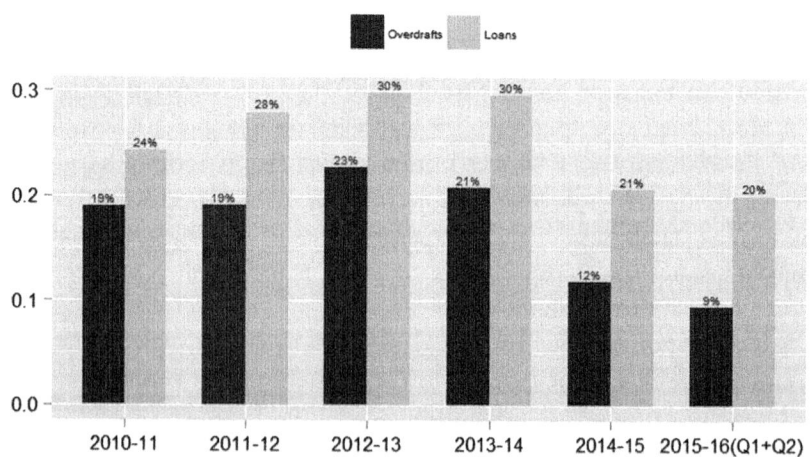

**Fig. 2.1** *Bank debt rejection rates by sub-periods. Note* Includes data on SMEs with bank debt applications. *Data source* UK SME Finance Monitor

**Table 2.1** Awareness of government initiatives by waves

| Government initiatives | Q3 2014 | Q4 2014 | Q1 2015 | Q2 2015 |
|---|---|---|---|---|
| FLS (%) | 30.5 | 30.1 | 28.5 | 29.3 |
| EFGS (%) | 24.8 | 22.7 | 21.8 | 21.0 |
| BGF (%) | 20.9 | 19.0 | 19.1 | 19.5 |
| BBB (%) | 14.5 | 13.2 | 12.9 | 14.4 |
| SLS (%) | 36.9 | 36.0 | 39.7 | 40.3 |
| Total (%) | 54.2 | 52.6 | 55.8 | 55.4 |
| No of observations | 5023 | 5024 | 5038 | 5001 |

*Note* Includes data on all SMEs.
*Data source* UK SME Finance Monitor

The figure presents the bank debt rejection rates by sub-periods. Two sets of observations can be made. First, rejection rates are consistently higher for loans compared to overdrafts. Second, for both overdrafts and loans, the rejection rates increase over the period, achieve their peak points and then start decreasing in 2013. A slight decrease appears in 2013–2014 for overdraft only, followed by a significant decline in 2014–2015. The levels of rejection rates during the last two sub-periods are remarkably lower than those during 2010–14. This kind of trend implies a tight credit condition after the most recent financial crisis till 2014 and suggests a potentially looser credit condition at present, for both overdrafts and loans.

Since 2014 Q3 (wave 14), the survey started to ask SMEs whether they were aware of any government initiatives, specifically:

Question 1: *Are you aware of any initiatives from government and other bodies to help make funding available to SMEs?*

Question 2: *More specifically, are you aware of... (multi-code)*

- *Funding for Lending*
- *Enterprise Finance Guarantee Scheme*
- *The Business Growth Fund*
- *The British Business Bank*
- *Start Up Loans*

Although only the data in the most recent four waves are available, it still gives us the opportunity to detect some trends in the awareness of government initiatives.

Table 2.1 shows the awareness of specific government initiatives by waves, and it also reports the proportion of SMEs aware of any of the public schemes. A downward trend can be found for the awareness of EFGS whereas more businesses were found to be aware of start-up loans opportunities (SLS). Compared with the proportion of SMEs aware of FLS or EFGS, more SMEs were aware of these two initiatives in 2015. In addition, more than half of the SMEs surveyed are aware of at least one of the government initiatives and the proportions in 2015 appear considerably higher than in the previous year.

## 2.4    Relationship Between Bank Debt Rejection Rates and Awareness of Government Initiatives

In this section, we analyse the relationship between rejection rates (for both overdrafts and loans) and awareness of government initiatives. First, charts will be presented that describe the rejection rates by the awareness of government initiatives. Then, statistical chi-square tests and correlation analysis will be conducted to check whether the differences are statistically significant and illustrate the strength of the association between these two variables.

As mentioned in Sect. 2.3, if SMEs are aware of government initiatives, they are likely to ultimately obtain better access to bank credit because they are generally more informed and, possibly, because the entrepreneurs are more financially literate. Figures 2.2 and 2.3 show the rejection rates by awareness of each government initiative for overdrafts and loans, respectively, with the first columns comparing the rejection rates of SMEs aware of *any* of the initiatives and SMEs aware of *none* of the initiatives. It appears that SMEs aware of any of the government initiatives usually have relatively lower rejection rates, compared with SMEs aware of none of the initiatives, indicating its positive effect on

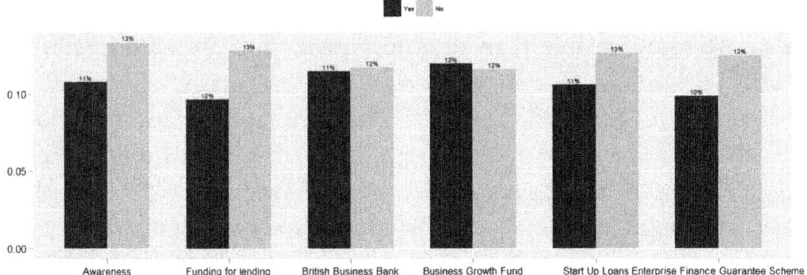

**Fig. 2.2** *Overdraft rejection rates by awareness of government initiatives. Note* Includes data on SMEs with overdraft applications from wave 14 (Q3 2014). *Data source* UK SME Finance Monitor

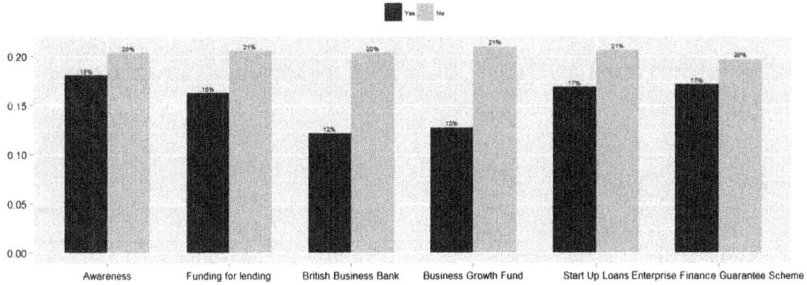

**Fig. 2.3** *Loan rejection rates by awareness of government initiatives, Note* Includes data on SMEs with loan applications from wave 14 (Q3 2014). *Data source* SME Finance Monitor

bank credit availability. Similar patterns can also be found for rejection rates by the awareness of FLS, SLS and EFGS. However, the awareness of BBB and BGF seems to have different effects on rejection rates for overdrafts and loans. Specifically, for overdrafts, there seems to be no difference between the rejection rates of SMEs aware and unaware of the initiative, whereas for loans, the counterpart differences become even larger than the differences for other three initiatives.

Among the possible reasons for the differences between overdrafts and loans in the awareness-rejection rate relationship are the different characteristics of the financial products that reflect the different margins that banks can make from the two debt financings.

Overdrafts facilities are typically renewed on an annual basis, they tend to be more flexible than term loans and they are used in the UK by small businesses to manage their short-term cash flow problems. As observed in Sect. 2.3, rejection rates are usually lower for overdrafts than for loans (see also Department for Business, Innovation and Skills 2016) not least because banks can take away an overdraft at short notice. Although overdrafts can be more expensive than loans, bank margins for overdrafts on average have been usually lower in the UK over the past 10 years (Armstrong et al. 2013). This reflects a lower level of control over the borrower, including perhaps their level of financial literacy.

Table 2.2 (panels a and b) displays the results for the chi-square tests between bank debt rejection rates and awareness of government initiatives. The results show that at least in three cases in both panels the relationship between awareness of specific government programmes and

**Table 2.2** Tests for differences

| Awareness of initiatives | Overdraft rejection rates | | Loan rejection rates | |
|---|---|---|---|---|
| | $\chi^2$ value | $p$-value | $\chi^2$ value | $p$-value |
| *Panel (a) Chi-square tests results* | | | | |
| FLS | **2.92** | 0.09 | 2.38 | 0.12 |
| EFGS | 1.82 | 0.18 | 0.68 | 0.41 |
| BGF | 0.01 | 0.92 | *7.29* | 0.01 |
| BBB | $6.47 \times 10^{-31}$ | 1.00 | *5.40* | 0.02 |
| SLS | 1.33 | 0.25 | 1.91 | 0.17 |
| Any | 1.93 | 0.16 | 0.60 | 0.44 |
| *Panel (b) Phi correlation coefficients* | | | | |
| | $\varphi$ coefficient | $p$-value | $\varphi$ coefficient | $p$-value |
| FLS | **−0.046** | 0.09 | −0.053 | 0.11 |
| EFGS | −0.037 | 0.15 | −0.030 | 0.36 |
| BGF | 0.005 | 0.85 | *−0.091* | 0.01 |
| BBB | −0.003 | 0.91 | *−0.079* | 0.01 |
| SLS | −0.032 | 0.22 | −0.048 | 0.14 |
| All | −0.038 | 0.14 | −0.028 | 0.39 |

*Note* **Bold** denotes significance at 10% level. **Bold** + *Italic* denotes significance at 5% level

rejection rates is statistically significant, albeit weak, at the 5% (BGF and BBB in the case of loans) and 10% (FLS in the case of overdrafts). However, when all programmes are tested, results for the differences appear insignificant so it will be useful to repeat the test when more waves of survey data become available.

## 2.5 Concluding Remarks

Due to the vital role that SMEs play in modern economies, issues around their access to bank credit have raised concerns for both academics, policy-makers and practitioners. In the aftermath of the most recent financial crisis, the UK government has launched several initiatives to encourage banks to extend lending to SMEs. This chapter utilises the SMEFM survey to investigate the relationship between bank credit availability and awareness of government initiatives.

The analysis carried out on the survey data on the UK's small businesses suggests that as time evolves, fewer SMEs are aware of Enterprise Finance Guarantee Schemes whereas more SMEs are aware of Start Up Loans Scheme. The data also provide some hints that UK SMEs that are aware of government initiatives are often less likely to be rejected when they apply for bank debt (overdrafts and loans). In particular, SMEs that are aware of Funding for Lending Schemes are less likely to experience overdraft rejections, and SMEs that are aware of Business Growth Funds or the British Business Bank are less likely to experience loan rejections. The study raises important questions on what could be the determinants of this awareness. One possible answer could be found in the level of financial literacy of the individual or individuals running the small businesses.

## Notes

1. Business Population Estimates of the Department for Business, Innovation & Skills (2013).
2. BDRC Continental: http://bdrc-continental.com/products/sme-finance-monitor/.

3. See Department for Business, Innovation and Skills (2013); the EFG is now wholly owned subsidiary of the British Business Bank plc.
4. For more details, see http://www.businessgrowthfund.co.uk.
5. For more information, please see http://british-business-bank.co.uk.
6. For more information, please see https://www.gov.uk/start-up-loans#what-you-need-to-know and https://www.startuploans.co.uk.
7. Financial literacy can be understood in the way that people's (or firms') "ability to process economic information and make informed decisions about financial planning, ..., debt, ..." (cited from Lusardi and Mitchell 2014, p. 6).
8. The first wave of the survey covered February–May 2011. From July 2011 onwards, the surveys were undertaken in standard quarter periods (i.e. January–March, April–June, July–September and October–December).

**Acknowledgements** The authors thank participants to the Wolpertinger Conference that was held at the University of Verona (Italy) in September 2016 and, in particular, the discussant Paola Bongini for useful comments and suggestions. The authors acknowledge support from grant number ES/L011859/1, from The Business and Local Government Data Research Centre, funded by the Economic and Social Research Council to provide researchers and analysts with secure data.

# References

Abor, J., and N. Biekpe. 2006. Small business financing initiatives in Ghana. *Problems and Perspectives in Management* 4 (3): 69–77.

Allinson, G., P. Robson, and I. Stone. 2013. Economic evaluation of the Enterprise Finance Guarantee (EFG) scheme. Report prepared for BIS, 1–80.

Armstrong, A., E.P. Davis, I. Liadze, and C. Rienzo. 2013. An assessment of bank lending to UK SMEs in the wake of the crisis. *National Institute Economic Review* 225 (1): R39–R51.

Bank of England. 2012. The funding for lending scheme. *Quarterly Bulletin* Q4: 306–320.

Bartoli, F., G. Ferri, P. Murro, and Z. Rotondi. 2013. Bank-firm relations and the role of mutual guarantee institutions at the peak of the crisis. *Journal of Financial Stability* 9 (1): 90–104.

Berger, A.N., and G.F. Udell. 2006. A more complete conceptual framework for SME finance. *Journal of Banking & Finance* 30 (11): 2945–2966.

Craig, B.R., W.E. Jackson, and J.B. Thomson. 2005. SBA-loan guarantees and local economic growth. Working Paper 05-03, The Federal Reserve Bank of Cleveland, 1–25.

Department for Business Innovation and Skills. 2013. *Understanding the Enterprise Finance Guarantee*. gov.uk.

Department for Business Innovation and Skills. 2016. SME lending and competition: An international comparison of markets. BIS Research Paper No. 270, May.

Fraser, S. 2012. The impact of the financial crisis on bank lending to SMEs. Report Prepared for BIS/Breedon Review, 1–68.

Hancock, D., J. Peek, and J.A. Wilcox. 2007. The repercussions on small banks and small businesses of procyclical bank capital and countercyclical loan guarantees. In *AFA 2008 New Orleans Meetings Paper,* 1–45.

Lusardi, A., and O.S. Mitchell. 2014. The economic importance of financial literacy: Theory and evidence. *Journal of Economic Literature* 52 (1): 5–44.

Rocha, R.D.R., S. Farazi, R. Khouri, and D. Pearce. 2011. The status of bank lending to SMES in the Middle East and North Africa region: The results of a joint survey of the Union of Arab Bank and the World Bank. World Bank Policy Research Working Paper Series, 1–57.

Storey, D.J. 1994. *Understanding the small business sector*. London: Routledge.

Udell, G.F. 2015. SME access to intermediated credit: What do we know and what don't we know? In *Small Business Conditions and Finance Conference Volume*.

Uesugi, I., K. Sakai, and G.M. Yamashiro. 2008. Effectiveness of credit guarantees in the Japanese loan market, 47–75.

Wilcox, J.A., and Y. Yasuda. 2008. Do government loan guarantees lower, or raise, banks' non-guaranteed lending? Evidence from Japanese banks. In *World Bank Workshop Partial Credit Guarantees,* March, 1–53.

Zecchini S., and M. Ventura. 2009. The impact of public guarantees on credit to SMEs. *Small Business Economics* 32 (2): 191–206.

## Authors' Biography

**Raffaella Calabrese** holds a B.Sc in Economics from Bocconi University (Italy) and a Ph.D. in Statistics from the University of Milan-Bicocca (Italy). Before joining the University of Edinburgh, Raffaella was a Lecturer at the

University of Essex. She has conducted research at the Wharton School of the University of Pennsylvania, Louisiana State University, Luigi Bocconi of Milan, University College Dublin and ETH Zurich. She has published widely on credit risk, systemic risk and rare events. Her research appears on journals such as *European Journal of Operational Research, Journal of Banking and Finance* and *Journal of Regional Science.*

**Claudia Girardone** is Professor of Banking and Finance and Director of the Essex Finance Centre at the Essex Business School of the University of Essex. Her current research interests are on banking sector performance and efficiency, bank corporate governance, SMEs' finance and the industrial structure of banking. She has published widely in the banking area and has recently co-authored the 2nd edition of the textbook Introduction to Banking (2015, Pearson). She is currently on the editorial board of several journals including the *Journal of Banking and Finance* and *The European Journal of Finance.*

**Mingchen Sun** is a Ph.D. student at the Essex Business School of the University of Essex. He holds a Master in Financial Engineering and Risk Management from the University of Essex and is part of the research team of the ESRC Business and Local Government Data Research Centre. His research interests include access to bank credit for SMEs' credit risk management and local banking market conditions.

# 3

# Earnings Quality and the Cost of Debt of SMEs

Federico Beltrame, Josanco Floreani and Alex Sclip

## 3.1 Introduction

This study examines whether earnings quality reduces information asymmetry and allows small and medium-sized enterprises (SMEs) to diminish the cost of debt. In the presence of information asymmetries, financial institutions face moral hazard and adverse selection problems, that make the assessment of the investment projects and the monitoring of their borrowers difficult. As a consequence, firms with higher information asymmetries obtain less debt financing with more stringent contractual terms. The consequences of information asymmetries are particularly relevant for SMEs. Given their higher levels of asymmetric information (Berger and Udell 1998), SMEs face more difficulties than

F. Beltrame (✉) · J. Floreani · A. Sclip
Department of Economics and Statistics, University of Udine, Udine, Italy
e-mail: federico.beltrame@uniud.it

© The Author(s) 2017
G. Chesini et al. (eds.), *Financial Markets, SME Financing and Emerging Economies*,
Palgrave Macmillan Studies in Banking and Financial Institutions,
DOI 10.1007/978-3-319-54891-3_3

large firms in accessing and obtaining financial resources from the capital markets (Titman and Wessels 1988).

The literature on SME financing has investigated the impact of asymmetric information as a determinant of bank debt from different perspectives. However, the role of the quality of financial statements in reducing information asymmetries in bank–firm debt contracting has not received much attention. For listed firms, information quality appears to be a factor that reduces information asymmetries faced by the lender as it improves the cost of debt financing (Francis et al. 2005), the maturity structure and the likelihood of providing collateral (Bharath et al. 2008). In contrast, for SMEs the precision of earnings improves the access (Garcìa-Teruel et al. 2014) and the cost (Vander Bauwhede et al. 2015) of bank debt.

Based on the previous research on the debt contracting consequences of earnings quality, this study aims to provide further evidence on the effects of accounting information quality on the cost of debt for a large sample of Italian SMEs.

To examine the impact of earnings quality on the cost of debt, we consider several proxies (Dechow and Dichev 2002; McNichols 2002; Pae 2011). Italian SMEs provide an interesting testing ground for our study. The industrial structure is, in fact, characterised by the large presence of small and medium-sized businesses with an almost exclusive dependence on bank financing as a source of external finance. In addition, in Italy information asymmetry problems arising to the quality of financial information are amplified by the regulatory framework[1] and the opaqueness of firm's financial positions (Berretta and Del Prete 2013).

This study adds to the SMEs literature in various ways. Firstly, notwithstanding a stream of research on earnings quality, as far as we are aware, only one study (Vander Bauwhede et al. 2015) investigates the link between earnings quality and the cost of debt for SMEs. Using a panel of Belgian SMEs over the years 1997–2010, the authors found that poorer earnings quality is associated with a higher interest cost. We therefore provide further insight into the matter by developing a cost-of-debt model based on the relevant drivers of SMEs' cost of debt. Secondly, our contribution is related to the geographical coverage and the size of the sample. To the best of our knowledge, it is the first study to estimate the relationship between information quality and the cost of debt for Italian SMEs. Moreover, previous studies on the effects of earnings quality on bank–firm access (Garcìa-Teruel et al. 2014; Vander Bauwhede et al. 2015) and cost of debt are based on a relatively small sample of firm-year observations.

Our findings show a negative association between our proxies of earnings quality and the cost of debt for SMEs, which suggest that earnings quality reduces information asymmetries and thus the cost of debt. These findings are important for both regulators and managers: for regulators, the results show that information quality is relevant for market participants. This implies that new rules might be set with the target of enhancing the quality of financial statements. For managers, our results suggest that the improvement of information quality has at least one economic benefit, as it reduces the cost of debt financing.

The chapter is organised as follows. The next section provides a literature review; Sect. 3.3 describes our data and the measures adopted in our analysis. Section 3.4 discusses our empirical results; and Sect. 3.5 concludes.

## 3.2   Literature Review

The main effect of information asymmetry between borrower and lender is to hinder a proper evaluation of firms and their projects, giving rise to adverse selection, moral hazard problems and eventually credit rationing (Stiglitz and Weiss 1981). Financial statements are central to the evaluation process of financial intermediaries. Banks use accounting information in order to estimate the expected future cash flows of the borrowers, and eventually the assessment of default risk (Berger and Udell 2006). Therefore, financial statements are an important source of information in mitigating the problems associated with borrower risk and information asymmetry.

As cash flows determine the ability to repay a loan, they are a central parameter in the pricing decision process. Prior research on earnings quality (Dechow et al. 1998) demonstrates that current earnings, as compared to current cash flows, are a more useful measure of firm performance that better predicts operating cash flows over short intervals. Accordingly, for creditors the higher the precision of earnings to capture future cash flows, the lower the information risk of the firm, due to the improved ability of the lender in estimating future cash flows of the firm with which the loans will be repaid. The superiority of earnings over cash flows in predicting future cash flows is that accruals shift the recognition of cash flows over time. However, the estimation process of accruals involves assumptions and estimates that could be biased (Dechow and Dichev 2002). Intentional and unintentional errors in the estimation of accruals reduce their beneficial role (Dechow and Dichev 2002). Hence, the quality of accruals and earnings is higher when they are less affected by estimation errors and are thus better able to predict future cash flows. The higher the quality of accruals, the higher the ability of creditors to make the right assessment of default risk and eventually reduce information asymmetry.

According to both theoretical (Easley and O'Hara 2004) and empirical studies on listed firms (Bharath et al. 2008; Francis et al. 2005), creditors price information risk as they charge a premium on firms with poorer reported financial statement quality. The underlying rational explanation of such effect is that information risk is non-diversifiable.

Accounting quality affects the choice of the debt market as well, with poorer accounting quality borrowers preferring bank loans (private debt) while higher accounting quality firms choosing the public debt markets (Bharath et al. 2008). This is consistent with the traditional view of credit intermediaries allowing an effective overcoming of adverse selection costs in debt contracts. Other evidence has shown that family firms obtain a lower pricing debt despite a low earnings quality because collateral and consolidated relations can reduce information asymmetries (Anderson et al. 2004). However, SMEs are riskier (Van Caneghem and Campenhout 2012) and present higher information risk (Ball and Shivakumar 2005) than listed firm; thus, the relationship between information risk and cost of capital might not hold. In addition, private debt markets suffer to a larger extent informational opacity (Van Caneghem and Campenhout 2012; Hernàndez-Cànovas and Martínez-Solano 2010).

To face the problems of SME lending market, banks use two main different lending technologies: transactional and relationship. According to Bartoli et al. (2013), Italian banks lend to SMEs by using both lending technologies, independently of the size and the proximity of the borrower. This framework leads to our empirical hypothesis that can be formulated as follows:

**H1** There is a negative association between financial reporting quality and the cost of debt for SMEs.

To support our hypothesis, we also acknowledge two recent papers of Garcìa-Teruel et al. (2014) and Vander Bauwhed et al. (2015). These papers focus on two different specific aspects of information quality. The former has demonstrated that earnings quality has a negative relationship with credit rationing for a panel of Spanish SMEs, while the second, which is the closest to our work, analyses the relationship between earnings quality and the cost of debt for Belgian SMEs, finding a negative association between information quality and the cost of debt. Both results of the papers support the financial literature which has shown that the use of bank debt is partially determined by information asymmetry. Moreover, we believe that the central role of accounting information in the transaction-based lending technology provides further supportive arguments of our hypothesis.

## 3.3   Sample and Data

Our sample contains financial information from non-financial Italian SMEs. The source of data is the Amadeus Database developed by Bureau Van Dijk, which contains accounting and financial information of European firms. We select industrial firms that during the period 2004–2012 satisfied the definition of medium-sized enterprises established by the European Commission recommendation 2003/361/EC: sales ranging from €10m to €50m, and range of total assets from 4.4 to 43 Mln €. We include in our sample medium-sized enterprises that satisfy both the requirements in terms of sales and assets defined above. We rely only on medium-sized enterprises because in Italy enterprises with total asset lower than 4.4 Mln € have the option to omit some details in their financial statements. Subsequently, we refined our data set by eliminating financial statements with inaccuracies in accounting data. The final panel data comprise 6707 medium-sized enterprises (25,963 firm-year observations over 2004–2012).

## 3.4  Research Design

### 3.4.1  Accruals Quality Metrics

We use three different proxies for accruals quality metrics, which have been employed in previous research. First, we use the model developed by Dechow and Dichev (2002). In this model, accruals quality is measured by their ability to map onto operating cash flows of the prior, current and next periods. The authors regress the current working capital accruals on cash flows from operations of the previous, the current and the next tax year. In the regression set-up, all the variables are divided by total assets.

$$\frac{WCA_{j,t}}{\text{Total Assets}_{i,t}} = \alpha_0 + \beta_1 \frac{CFO_{j,t-1}}{\text{Total Assets}_{i,t}} + \beta_2 \frac{CFO_{j,t}}{\text{Total Assets}_{i,t}}$$
$$+ \beta_3 \frac{CFO_{j,t+1}}{\text{Total Assets}_{i,t}} + \varepsilon_{j,t} \tag{3.1}$$

where $WCA_{j,t}$ is working capital accruals of firm $j$ in year $t$, calculated as the change in current assets ($\Delta CA$), minus the change in current liabilities ($\Delta CL$), minus the change in cash ($\Delta Cash$), plus the change in short-term bank debt ($\Delta STDEB$). $CFO_{j,t-1}$, $CFO_{j,t}$ and $CFO_{j,t+1}$ are cash flow from operations of firm $j$ in year $t-1$, $t$ and $t + 1$, respectively, calculated as net income before extraordinary (**NIBE**) items in year $t$ minus total accruals (TA). Total accruals are calculated as a difference of working capital accruals minus depreciation and amortisation expenses (Depn).

The second proxy for accruals quality is the Dechow and Dichev (2002) model, modified by McNichols (2002), which includes changes in revenues ($\Delta$Revenues) and property plant and equipment (PPE) as independent variables.

$$
\begin{aligned}
\frac{\text{WCA}_{i,t}}{\text{Total Assets}_{i,t}} &= \alpha_0 + \beta_1 \frac{\Delta\text{Revenues}_{j,t}}{\text{Total Assets}_{i,t}} + \beta_2 \frac{\text{PPE}_{j,t}}{\text{Total Assets}_{i,t}} \\
&+ \beta_3 \frac{\text{CFO}_{j,t-1}}{\text{Total Assets}_{i,t}} + \beta_4 \frac{\text{CFO}_{j,t}}{\text{Total Assets}_{i,t}} \\
&+ \beta_5 \frac{\text{CFO}_{j,t+1}}{\text{Total Assets}_{i,t}} + \varepsilon_{j,t}
\end{aligned}
\tag{3.2}
$$

Our third proxy is the accruals quality model developed by Pae (2011). Different from the Dechow and Dichev (2002) and the McNichols (2002) models described above, it takes into account only cash flows from previous years.

$$
\begin{aligned}
\frac{\text{WCA}_{i,t}}{\text{Total Assets}_{i,t}} &= \alpha_0 + \beta_1 \frac{\Delta\text{Sales}_{j,t}}{\text{Total Assets}_{i,t}} + \beta_2 \frac{\text{PPE}_{j,t}}{\text{Total Assets}_{i,t}} \\
&+ \beta_3 \frac{\text{CFO}_{j,t-2}}{\text{Total Assets}_{i,t}} + \beta_4 \frac{\text{CFO}_{j,t-1}}{\text{Total Assets}_{i,t}} \\
&+ \beta_5 \frac{\text{CFO}_{j,t}}{\text{Total Assets}_{i,t}} + \varepsilon_{j,t}
\end{aligned}
\tag{3.3}
$$

The accruals quality proxies that we use are based on the standard deviation of the residuals of the previous models estimated in Eq. (3.1) ($\text{AQ}_{dd} = \sigma\left(\varepsilon_{i,t}\right)$), Eq. (3.2) ($\text{AQ}_{mc} = \sigma\left(\varepsilon_{i,t}\right)$) and Eq. (3.3) ($\text{AQ}_{pae} = \sigma\left(\varepsilon_{i,t}\right)$), respectively. The residual standard deviation is an inverse measure of accruals quality for firm $j$ in year $t$, calculated over periods $t-3$ to $t$.

## 3.4.2 Model Specification

The next step in our empirical analysis is to analyse the relationship between the cost of debt and accruals quality. To do so, we regress the cost of debt against the accruals quality metric and a set of independent variables related to the firms' characteristics. The regression formula is the following:

$$
\begin{aligned}
\text{Cost of Debt}_{j,t} = {} & \alpha_0 + \beta_1 \text{AQ}_{j,t} + \beta_2 \frac{\text{SF}_{j,t}}{\text{TL}_{j,t}} + \beta_3 \frac{\text{LT Debt}_{j,t}}{\text{TL}_{j,t}} + \beta_4 \text{ROA}_{j,t} \\
& + \beta_5 \frac{\text{IE}_{j,t}}{\text{Revenues}_{j,t}} \beta_6 \frac{\text{Fixed Assets}_{j,t}}{\text{TA}_{j,t}} \\
& + \beta_7 \frac{\text{CFO}_{j,t}}{\text{Investments}_{j,t}} + \beta_8 \frac{\text{Credits}_{j,t}}{\text{TA}_{j,t}} + \beta_9 \text{Size}_{j,t} \\
& + \beta_{10} \text{Policy rates}_t \\
& + \beta_{11} \text{Default Dummy}_{j,t} + \varepsilon_{j,t}
\end{aligned}
\tag{3.4}
$$

where Cost of debt represents the ratio of interest expenses to financial debts; AQ is the accruals quality proxy; SF/TL is the ratio of shareholders' funds to total liabilities; LT Debt/TL is the ratio of long-term debt to total liabilities; ROA is return on assets; IE/Revenues stands for the ratio of interest expenses to revenues; Fixed Assets/TA is the ratio of fixed assets to total assets; CFO/Investments represents the cash flow from operations to investments; Credits/TA is commercial credits over total assets; Size is the log of total assets; Policy rates represents the average cost of money in Italian banking sector; Default dummy level represents a dummy variable set to 1 in years in which firm $j$ is near the default level, zero otherwise. The default level is calculated using the Altman zeta-score indicator readapted for Italian companies in Altman et al. (2013).

Firm-level control variables are based on prior studies that have examined credit risk of SMEs (Minnis 2011; Hernández-Cánovas and Martínez-Solano 2007; Altman et al. 2008). These are the ratio of shareholders' funds to total liabilities, the ratio of long-term debt to total liabilities, the cash flow from operations to investments, ROA, the ratio of interest expenses to revenues, the level of commercial credits to total assets and the size.

The ratio of capital to total liabilities represents the capital structure of the company. Since financial risk increased in leverage, it is expected that more leveraged firms pay a higher average interest rate. But, also negative leverage coefficients have been found in the academic literature (Minnis 2011; Francis et al. 2005; Booth 1992), a result that is in line with the hypothesis that firms that are offered loans at attractive interest rates are more likely to borrow larger amounts. Thus, we have no prediction about the sign of the coefficient of this variable.

The ratio of long-term financial debt to total debt represents the maturity composition of the financial debt. Firms with a higher portion of long-term debt are less prone to fail (Altman et al. 2008). ROA indicates profitability and profitable firms are expected to lower the probability of financial distress and thus the cost of debt. The ratio of interest expenses to revenues represents the ability to pay interest on outstanding debt. We predict a negative sign of this variable, since a substantial ability to pay interest on outstanding debt lowers the firm's financial distress probability. Fixed assets divided by total assets is used as a proxy of asset tangibility. Higher values of asset tangibility are likely to be associated with a lower financial risk (Vander Bauwhede et al. 2015). Cash flows to investments represent the ability of cash flow to servicing investments. We expect a negative sign for this variable, since expensive investments typically need high cash flows. We also control for the ability to redeem commercial credits with the variable ratio of commercial credits to total assets. Higher levels denote lower ability of transforming credits into cash, which rises the probability of failure. Size is measured by the logarithm of total assets and is expected to be negatively related to the cost of debt. Finally, we add two control variables. The first is the average cost of funds for Italian banks (Source: Bank of Italy), which obviously affects the cost of debt for SMEs. The second control variable is a dummy that takes the value of 1 when a firm is in a default state and zero otherwise. We use this variable because the dynamic of interest expense rate could differ between default and non-default debtors.

## 3.5    Results

### 3.5.1    Descriptive Statistics

Table 3.1 summarises the descriptive statistics for the variables used in our empirical investigation. In our sample, the mean cost of debt is 6.1% and the average ratio of shareholders' funds to total assets is 23%. On average, firms in the sample are profitable (mean ROA 5.3%) and the ratio of fixed assets to total asset is 25%. The lower ratio of shareholder funds to total liabilities highlighted the importance of bank debt for Italian medium-sized enterprises.

**Table 3.1** Descriptive statistics

| Variable | Mean | 1°Quartile | Median | 3°Quartile | Standard deviation |
|---|---|---|---|---|---|
| *Earnings quality metrics* | | | | | |
| $AQ_{dd}$ | 0.012 | 0.006 | 0.011 | 0.020 | 0.215 |
| $AQ_{mcn}$ | 0.014 | 0.006 | 0.012 | 0.021 | 0.160 |
| $AQ_{pae}$ | 0.013 | 0.006 | 0.012 | 0.020 | 0.149 |
| *Financial variables* | | | | | |
| Cost of debt | 0.061 | 0.037 | 0.052 | 0.072 | 0.037 |
| SF/TL | 0.232 | 0.119 | 0.203 | 0.319 | 0.145 |
| LT Debt/TL | 0.069 | 0.000 | 0.029 | 0.110 | 0.093 |
| ROA | 0.053 | 0.020 | 0.042 | 0.078 | 0.045 |
| IE/Revenues | 0.014 | 0.003 | 0.008 | 0.016 | 0.051 |
| Fixed assets/TA | 0.255 | 0.093 | 0.217 | 0.374 | 0.176 |
| CFO/Investments | 0.022 | −0.049 | 0.065 | 0.200 | 0.370 |
| Credits/TA | 0.287 | 0.166 | 0.263 | 0.386 | 0.142 |
| Size | 4.064 | 3.880 | 4.072 | 4.262 | 0.254 |
| Policy rates | 0.015 | 0.013 | 0.013 | 0.016 | 0.002 |

This table shows the summary statistics of the variables used in our empirical analysis. $AQ_{dd}$ is the Dechow and Dichev (2002) proxy of accruals quality. $AQ_{mcn}$ is the accruals quality proxy developed by McNichols (2002). $AQ_{pae}$ is the accruals quality proxy as defined in Pae (2011). Cost of debt represents the ratio of interest expenses to financial debts; SF/TL is the ratio of shareholders' funds to total liabilities; LT Debt/TL is the ratio of long-term debt to total liabilities; CFO/Investments represents the cash flow from operations to investments; ROA is return on assets; Fixed assets/TA is the ratio of fixed assets to total assets; IE/Revenues stands for the ratio of interest expenses to revenues; Credits/TA is commercial credits over total assets; Size is the log of total assets; Policy rates represents the average cost of money in Italian banking sector

**Table 3.2** Correlation matrix

| | AQ_dd | AQ_mcn | AQ_Pae | Cost of debt | SF/TL | LT Debt/TL | ROA | IE/Revenues | Fixed Assets/TA | CFO/Investments | Credits/TA | Size | Policy Rates | Default Dummy |
|---|---|---|---|---|---|---|---|---|---|---|---|---|---|---|
| AQ_dd | 1 | | | | | | | | | | | | | |
| AQ_mcn | 0.318*** | 1 | | | | | | | | | | | | |
| AQ_Pae | 0.101 | 0.709*** | 1 | | | | | | | | | | | |
| Cost of Debt | 0.044 | 0.0367*** | 0.061*** | 1 | | | | | | | | | | |
| SF/TL | 0.023*** | 0.0596*** | 0.0215** | -0.038*** | 1 | | | | | | | | | |
| LT Debt/TL | 0.001 | -0.005 | -0.006 | -0.170*** | -0.104*** | 1 | | | | | | | | |
| ROA | 0.016** | 0.027*** | 0.048*** | 0.137*** | 0.137*** | -0.041*** | 1 | | | | | | | |
| IE/Revenues | -0.011* | -0.015** | 0.001 | 0.209*** | -0.209*** | 0.305*** | -0.067*** | 1 | | | | | | |
| Fixed Assets/TA | 0.022** | 0.009* | -0.007 | -0.082*** | -0.082*** | 0.355*** | -0.085*** | 0.093*** | 1 | | | | | |
| CFO/Investments | 0.0127* | 0.0167*** | 0.038*** | -0.018* | 0.074*** | -0.018* | 0.096*** | -0.0641*** | 0.071*** | 1 | | | | |
| Credits/TA | -0.022** | -0.064*** | -0.039*** | 0.214*** | -0.44*** | -0.270*** | -0.013* | -0.311*** | -0.346*** | 0.064*** | 1 | | | |
| Size | -0.015** | -0.034*** | -0.052*** | -0.171*** | 0.21*** | 0.089*** | -0.121*** | 0.239*** | 0.157*** | -0.0136** | -0.323*** | 1 | | |
| Policy Rates | -0.0001 | -0.004 | -0.020*** | 0.207*** | -0.102*** | -0.002 | 0.162*** | 0.082*** | -0.055*** | -0.046*** | 0.084*** | -0.052*** | 1 | |
| Default Dummy | -0.010* | -0.012* | -0.009 | -0.128*** | 0.083*** | 0.214*** | -0.381*** | 0.361*** | 0.336*** | -0.051*** | -0.322*** | 0.375*** | -0.071*** | 1 |

* denotes significance at the 10% level, ** denotes significance at the 5% level and *** denotes significance at the 1% level

Table 3.2 presents the Pearson correlation matrix between the variables used in the empirical model. As expected, the accruals quality metric shows a positive correlation with the cost of debt. Taking into account that higher values of the accruals quality metric denote poorer quality, the correlation matrix results show preliminary evidence of a negative association between accruals quality and cost of debt. Consistent with García-Teruel et al. (2014), our matrix of correlation suggests a negative correlation between accruals quality and the leverage ratio.

## 3.5.2 Regression Results

In Table 3.3, we show the results of our regression model (2). We present results for the three measures of accruals quality defined above, using fixed-effects estimator.

The estimated coefficients of AQ are significant and have a positive sign. Since higher values for the AQ are associated with poorer earnings quality, these results provide evidence that accruals quality diminishes the cost of debt of Italian SMEs. These findings are consistent with the previous works of Bharath et al. (2008), Francis et al. (2004) and Vander Bauwhede et al. (2015).

The leverage coefficient is positive and significant, consistent with Minnis (2011), Francis et al. (2005) and Booth (1992). Two main

Table 3.3  Accruals quality and the cost of debt

| | (1) | (2) | (3) | (4) |
|---|---|---|---|---|
| AQ$_{dd}$ | | 0.019* | | |
| | | (2.128) | | |
| AQ$_{mcn}$ | | | 0.025* | |
| | | | (2.27) | |
| AQ$_{pae}$ | | | | 0.098*** |
| | | | | (5.123) |
| SF/TL | 0.047*** | 0.047*** | 0.046*** | 0.046*** |
| | (13.684) | (12.749) | (12.821) | (12.799) |
| LT debt/TL | −0.061*** | −0.062*** | −0.062*** | −0.062*** |
| | (−19.851) | (−18.917) | (−18.700) | (−18.766) |
| ROA | 0.086*** | 0.086*** | 0.086*** | 0.089*** |
| | (17.305) | (15.842) | (15.770) | (16.381) |
| IE/Revenues | 1.494*** | 1.562*** | 1.560*** | 1.556*** |
| | (19.038) | (17.944) | (17.966) | (17.983) |
| Fixed assets/TA | 0.015*** | 0.018*** | 0.017*** | 0.018*** |
| | (7.678) | (8.868) | (8.785) | (8.943) |
| CFO/Investments | −0.004*** | −0.004*** | −0.003*** | −0.004*** |
| | (−5.085) | (−4.578) | (−4.574) | (−4.607) |
| Credits/TA | 0.081*** | 0.0757*** | 0.076*** | 0.077*** |
| | (20.979) | (19.351) | (19.375) | (19.505) |
| Size | −0.028*** | −0.029*** | −0.028*** | −0.028*** |
| | (−20.979) | (−19.685) | (−19.570) | (−19.235) |
| Policy rates | 1.823*** | 1.303*** | 1.306*** | 1.314*** |
| | (28.171) | (17.535) | (17.567) | (17.703) |
| Default dummy | −0.006*** | −0.006*** | −0.006*** | −0.006*** |
| | (−13.163) | (17.535) | (−13.839) | (−13.754) |
| Constant | 0.094*** | 0.105*** | 0.104*** | 0.100*** |
| | (15.811) | (17.289) | (17.003) | (16.532) |
| Observations | 31190 | 25986 | 25963 | 25963 |
| $R^2$ | 0.337 | 0.310 | 0.311 | 0.312 |

The regressions have been carried out using the fixed-effects estimator. Standard errors are robust to heteroscedasticity. t-statistics in brackets. * denotes significance at the 10% level, ** denotes significance at the 5% level, and *** denotes significance at the 1% level

reasons might explain the sign. Firstly, according to Minnis (2011), the positive sign has an econometric cause as it is possibly driven by the negative correlation between leverage and interest expenses to total revenues (−0.209, $p < 0.01$). Secondly, Booth (1992) claims that there might be economies of scale in lending. We find supporting evidence for this idea as larger companies of our sample are more levered and are typically characterised by a lower cost of debt. The negative sign of long-term debt over total debt confirms agency theory hypothesis that claims that shorter maturities and higher leverage rise the cost of debt, due to the information asymmetry problems. Furthermore, the effect is justified because the long-term debt tends to be cheaper than the short one. Contrary to our expectations, the ROA coefficient enters a positive and significant sign. The reasons could be related to amortisations included in the formula counter and the differences in banking credit evaluation. In addition, the Italian banking system is characterised by a large number of small local banks that consider firms' capital consistency and collaterals as more important than a firm's yield. As expected, interest coverage has a significant positive sign, suggesting that a higher incidence of interest rates on revenues increases the probability of failure and thus the cost of debt of the companies.

Asset tangibility has a positive impact on the cost of debt because it could be used as a proxy of collateral: the higher the presence of fixed assets, the grater the collateral availability. Cash flows to investments have the expected sign, since expensive investments need high cash flows to serve these investments.

With respect to the remaining significant control variables, credits to total assets and size have the expected sign. For the cost of funds, we find, as expected, a significantly positive coefficient. The default dummy variable also has the predicted sign, suggesting that banks do not rise interest rates to firms near the default state.

A possible limitation of our study is that we do not take into consideration the role of soft variables in the empirical model. Soft variables are relevant in the assessment of SMEs' creditworthiness process; however, the use of soft variables depends on the size of the financial intermediary and the bank–firm relationship (Berger et al. 2001, 2005). This should imply further analysis on the type of banks and their characteristics.

However, previous studies suggested that the quality of earnings is associated with a number of different factors, such as ownership structure (Wang 2006), human capital (Darabi et al. 2012), management ability (Demerjian et al. 2012) and the degree of business innovation, which are together soft variables used by banks in the assessment of the creditworthiness process. Therefore, we believe that the inclusion of those variables in our regression framework reinforces the relationship between accruals quality and the cost of debt.

### 3.5.3 Robustness Test

Dechow and Dichev (2002) distinguished between innate factors and discretionary factors in the accruals quality metric. Innate factors are those related to firm characteristics such as the business model and the operating environment, while discretionary factors are those associated with financial reporting discretion of managers. Francis et al. (2005) successfully distinguished the effect of both factors on the cost of capital of listed US firms. We also control for the innate portion of accruals identified by Dechow and Dichev (2002) as control variables, and we find results consistent with those displayed in Table 3.3.

According to Dechow et al. (1996) and Gosh and Moon (2010), a potential motivation for earnings manipulation is to avoid debt covenant violation. Therefore, high-leveraged firms are more likely to engage in earnings manipulation practices, which are expected to reduce the quality of financial statement information.

We address this potential endogeneity problem by using a two-stage least squares model. Accruals quality is estimated endogenously in the first-stage regression, and the cost of debt is the dependent variable in the second-stage regression. In the first stage, we estimate accruals quality with the following model:

$$
\begin{aligned}
\text{AQ}_{i,t} = {} & \text{Intercept} + \gamma_1 \text{Size}_{i,t} + \gamma_2 \text{OperCycle}_{i,t} + \gamma_3 \sigma(\text{Sales})_{i,t} \\
& + \gamma_4 \sigma(\text{CFO})_{i,t} + \gamma_5 \text{NegEarn}_{i,t} + \gamma_6 \text{DCG} \\
& + \gamma_7 \frac{\text{SF}_{j,t}}{\text{TL}_{j,t}}{}_{i,t} + \eta_i + \lambda_t + \varepsilon_{i,to}
\end{aligned}
\tag{3.5}
$$

where OperCycle is the length of operating cycle, $\sigma(\text{Sales})$ is the standard deviation of sales, $\sigma(\text{CFO})$ is the standard deviation of cash from operations, NegEarn is the number of years in which earnings are negative and DCG is a dummy variable which takes value 1 in the presence of an external auditor.

We add this variable because external auditors prevent earnings management actions and diminished information risk (Lin and Hwang 2010).

In the second stage, we use the predicted value of accruals quality from the first-stage regression. The results of the 2SLS model are displayed in Table 3.4 and basically confirm our main findings. Accruals quality metrics are negatively and significantly related to the cost of debt.

**Table 3.4** Accruals quality and the cost of debt: two-stage regressions

|  | (1) | (2) | (3) |
|---|---|---|---|
| $AQ_{dd}$ | −0.098 | | |
|  | (−1.13) | | |
| $AQ_{mcn}$ | | 0.025** | |
|  | | (2.22) | |
| $AQ_{pae}$ | | | 0.097*** |
|  | | | (7.87) |
| SF/TL | 0.048*** | 0.048*** | 0.047*** |
|  | (22.37) | (22.41) | (22.29) |
| LT debt/TL | −0.060*** | −0.061*** | −0.060*** |
|  | (−23.38) | (−23.21) | (−23.24) |
| ROA | 0.085*** | 0.086*** | 0.088*** |
|  | (20.32) | (20.24) | (20.25) |
| IE/Revenues | 1.564*** | 1.567*** | 1.563*** |
|  | (85.41) | (85.39) | (85.26) |
| Fixed assets/TA | 0.018*** | 0.018*** | 0.018*** |
|  | (11.08) | (11.02) | (11.15) |
| CFO/Investments | −0.004*** | −0.004*** | −0.005*** |
|  | (−9.95) | (−9.98) | (−10.30) |
| Credits/TA | 0.077*** | 0.077*** | 0.077*** |
|  | (35.69) | (35.70) | (35.88) |
| Size | −0.029*** | −0.029*** | −0.029*** |
|  | (−24.90) | (−24.78) | (−24.39) |
| Policy rates | 1.313*** | 1.316*** | 1.324*** |
|  | (15.10) | (15.12) | (15.22) |
| Default dummy | −0.006*** | −0.006*** | −0.006*** |
|  | (−15.63) | (−15.70) | (−15.64) |
| Constant | 0.106*** | 0.105*** | 0.102*** |
|  | (21.09) | (20.83) | (20.18) |
| Observations | 25491 | 25443 | 25443 |

The regressions have been estimated using the fixed-effects estimator. Standard errors are robust to heteroscedasticity. t-statistics in brackets. * denotes significance at the 10% level, ** denotes significance at the 5% level, and *** denotes significance at the 1% level

## 3.6  Conclusions

In this chapter, we provide a detailed investigation of the relationship between accruals quality and cost of debt in SMEs. Our results demonstrate that information risk rises the cost of debt for SMES, and they are broadly in line with those obtained by Francis et al. (2005) for listed firms and Vander Bauwhede et al. (2015) for 2692 Belgian SMEs.

Our empirical evidence also confirms a link between financial structure, earnings quality and information asymmetry. In line with Gosh and Moon (2010) and Fung and Goodwin (2013), we find that earnings quality is negatively related to leverage and debt maturity structure.

Our results are consistent with the view that earnings are important for banks in assessing the creditworthiness of SMEs, and less estimation errors in accruals enhance the ability of earnings to predict future cash flows.

These results are valuable for SMEs' managers since they emphasise the economic benefits of financial reporting quality. To the extent that opportunistic earnings management reduces accruals quality, managers can learn that managing earnings have the potential disadvantage of increasing interest expenses. The results are also important for regulators. To the extent that managerial discretion can impair accounting information, our results suggest stricter accounting rules as this may reduce information asymmetries between SMEs and their creditors.

## Note

1. The Italian law permits the option to omit details in financial statements for firms with the following characteristics: total assets lower than €4.4m, revenues lower than €8.8m and less than 50 employees.

## References

Altman, E.I., G. Sabato, and N. Wilson. 2008. The value of qualitative information in SME risk management. *Journal of Financial Services Research* 40 (2): 15–55.

Altman, E.I., A. Danovi, and A. Falini. 2013. Z-score models' application to Italian companies subject to extraordinary administration. *Journal of Applied Finance* 23 (1): 1–10.

Anderson, R.C., S.A. Mansi, and D.M. Reeb. 2004. Board characteristics, accounting report integrity, and the cost of debt. *Journal of Accounting and Economics* 37 (3): 315–342.

Ball, R., and L. Shivakumar. 2005. Earnings quality in UK private firms: Comparative loss recognition timeliness. *Journal of Accounting and Economics* 39 (1): 83–128.

Bartoli, F., G. Ferri, P. Murro, and Z. Rotondi. 2013. SME financing and the choice of lending technology in Italy: Complementarity or substitutability? *Journal of Banking & Finance* 37: 5476–5485.

Berger, A.N., and G.F. Udell. 1998. The economics of small business finance: The roles of private equity and debt markets in the financial growth cycle. *Journal of Banking & Finance* 22 (6): 613–673.

Berger, A.N., L. Klapper, and G. Udell. 2001. The ability of banks to lend to informationally opaque small businesses. *Journal of Banking & Finance* 25: 2127–2167.

Berger, A.N., N.H. Miller, M.A. Petersen, R.G. Rajan, and J.C. Stein. 2005. Does function follow organizational form? Evidence from the lending practices of large and small banks. *Journal of Financial Economics* 76 (2): 237–269.

Berger, A.N., and G.F. Udell. 2006. A more complete conceptual framework for SME finance. *Journal of Banking & Finance* 30 (11): 2945–2966.

Berretta, E., and S. Del Prete. 2013. Banking consolidation and bank-firm credit relationship: The role of geographical features and relationship characteristics. (Bank of Italy, Working paper, No. 901).

Bharath, S.T., J. Sunder, and S.V. Sunder. 2008. Accounting quality and debt contracting. *The Accounting Review* 83 (1): 1–28.

Booth, J.R. 1992. Contract costs, bank loans, and the cross-monitoring hypothesis. *Journal of Financial Economics* 31 (1): 25–41.

Darabi, R., K. Rad, and M. Ghadiri. 2012. The relationship between intellectual capital and earnings quality. *Research Journal of Applied Sciences, Engineering and Technology* 4: 4192–4199.

Dechow, P., R. Sloan, and A. Sweeney. 1996. Causes and consequences of earnings manipulation: An analysis of firm subject to enforcement actions by the SEC. *Contemporary Accounting Research* 13: 1–36.

Dechow, P.M., and I.D. Dichev. 2002. The quality of accruals and earnings: The role of accrual estimation errors. *The Accounting Review* 77 (s-1): 35–59.

Dechow, P.M., S.P. Kothari, and R.L. Watts. 1998. The relation between earnings and cash flows. *Journal of Accounting and Economics* 25 (2): 133–168.

Demerjian, P.R., B. Lev, M.F. Lewis, and S.E. McVay. 2012. Managerial ability and earnings quality. *The Accounting Review* 88(2): 463–498.

Easley, D., and M. O'Hara. 2004. Information and the cost of capital. *The Journal of Finance* 59 (4): 1553–1583.

Francis, J., R. Lafond, and K. Schipper. 2004. Costs of equity and earnings attributes. *The Accounting Review* 79 (4): 967–1010.

Francis, J., R. LaFond, P. Olsson, and K. Schipper. 2005. The market pricing of accruals quality. *Journal of Accounting and Economics* 39 (2): 295–327.

Fung, S.Y., and J. Goodwin. 2013. Short-term debt maturity, monitoring and accruals-based earnings management. *Journal of Contemporary Accounting & Economics* 9 (1): 67–82.

García-Teruel, P.J., P. Martínez-Solano, and J.P. Sánchez-Ballesta. 2014. The role of accruals quality in the access to bank debt. *Journal of Banking & Finance* 38: 186–193.

Gosh, A., and D. Moon. 2010. Corporate Debt Financing and Earnings Quality. *Journal of Business Finance & Accounting* 37: 538–559.

Hernández-Cánovas, G., and P. Martínez-Solano. 2007. Effect of the number of banking relationships on credit availability: Evidence from panel data of Spanish small firms. *Small Business Economics* 28 (1): 37–53.

Hernández-Cánovas, G., and P. Martínez-Solano. 2010. Relationship lending and SME financing in continental European bank-based system. *Small Business Economics* 34 (4): 465–482.

Lin, J.W., and M.I. Hwang. 2010. Audit quality, corporate governance, and earnings management: A meta analysis. *International Journal of Auditing* 14 (1): 57–77.

McNichols, M.F. 2002. Discussion of the quality of accruals and earnings: The role of accrual estimation errors. *The Accounting Review* 77 (s-1): 61–69.

Minnis, M. 2011. The value of financial statement verification in debt financing: Evidence from private U.S. firms. *Journal of Accounting Research* 49 (2): 457–506.

Pae, J. 2011. A synthesis of accrual quality and abnormal accrual models: An empirical implementation. *Asia-Pacific Journal of Accounting & Economics* 18 (1): 27–44.

Stiglitz, J.E., and A. Weiss. 1981. Credit rationing in markets with imperfect information. *The American Economic Review* 71 (3): 393–410.

Titman, S., and R. Wessels. 1988. The Determinants of Capital Structure Choice. *The Journal of Finance* 43 (1): 1–19.

Van Caneghem, T., and G. Campenhout. 2012. Quantity and quality of information and SME financial structure. *Small Business Economics* 39 (2): 341–358.

Van der Bauwhede, H., M. De Meyere, and P. Van Cauwenberge. 2015. Financial reporting quality and the cost of debt of SMEs. *Small Business Economics* 45 (1): 149–164.

Wang, D. 2006. Founding family ownership and earnings quality. *Journal of Accounting Research* 44 (3): 619–656.

# Authors' Biography

**Federico Beltrame** is Lecturer in Banking and Finance in the Department of Economics and Statistics, University of Udine, where he teaches corporate finance. He graduated in Economics at the University of Udine, where he also received his Ph.D. in Business Science. His main research interests are related to SMEs' cost of capital, banks' capital structure and mutual guarantee credit institutions.

**Josanco Floreani** is Associate Professor in Corporate Finance in the Department of Economics and Statistics, University of Udine. He graduated in Economics at the University of Udine, where he also received his Ph.D. His main research interests are related to firm's financial performances and governance and Islamic Finance.

**Alex Sclip** is a Ph.D. student in Banking and Finance at the Department of Economics and Statistics, University of Udine. His research topics include capital structure and risk management in banking and insurance.

# 4

# Demand and Supply Determinants of Credit Availability: Evidence from the Current Credit Crisis for European SMEs

Paola Brighi and Valeria Venturelli

## 4.1 Introduction

The recent financial crisis has renewed the interest for credit rationing since many firms, becoming more vulnerable because of the crisis, meet problems in access to credit. This is particularly relevant for small and medium-sized enterprises (SMEs) and for more bank-oriented countries. As suggested by the pecking-order theory (Myers and Majluf 1984), SMEs are more financially constrained than large firms because they are more opaque (Berger and Udell 1998; Cole et al. 2004). This opaqueness increases in the case of young and innovative firms (Berger and Udell 1998) implying that self-financing is their dominant financial

P. Brighi
Department of Management, University of Bologna, Bologna, Italy

V. Venturelli (✉)
Department of Economics Marco Biagi, University of Modena and Reggio Emilia, Modena, Italy
e-mail: valeria.venturelli@unimore.it

© The Author(s) 2017                                                              **41**
G. Chesini et al. (eds.), *Financial Markets, SME Financing and Emerging Economies*,
Palgrave Macmillan Studies in Banking and Financial Institutions,
DOI 10.1007/978-3-319-54891-3_4

source, followed among the external finance categories, by private equity and venture capital and then by bank loans.

On the bank side, the financial crisis  has exacerbated the credit selection criteria with severe effects in terms of credit supply restrictions. According to the responses provided by the euro-area banks participating at the Eurosystem Bank Lending Survey, a rapid tightening of supply conditions occurred at the start of 2009. Further evidence, conducted by the ECB together with the European Commission, suggests that conditions of access to credit continued to tighten in the second part of 2009, especially for SMEs. However, the trend in access to credit to the private sector differs considerably from country to country within the euro area (Bank of Italy, Annual Report Bank of Italy 2010, p. 46).

In this respect, the aim of this contribution is to investigate the reasons of demand and supply factors of credit constraints within some principal European countries. In order to investigate our main research questions, we use data from the "European Firms in a Global Economy" (EFIGE) survey, which provides comparative data on European manufacturing firms. We test the determinants of credit demand; then, we test for the effect of financial constraints by using direct binary indicators of credit rationing, based on survey responses.

As the SMEs' economic and financial conditions worsened because of the crisis, banks that based their selection criteria to some extent on hard information were forced to tighten credit offer. Consequently, SMEs—more credit rationed—reduced at least partly their investment with a negative impact in terms of credit demand. However, how credit demand and supply schedules reach a new equilibrium/disequilibrium condition strongly depend also on the bank–firm relationship intensity. In this respect, the main research question of this contribution is to investigate how a mix of factors characterizing both country financial systems—bank or market oriented— and SMEs' financing structure and their bank attitude may affect the final credit-rationing condition.

Our analysis offers three main contributions to the existing literature. Firstly, as almost all studies consist in single-country analyses (see, among others, Kremp and Sevestre 2013; Kirschenmann 2016; Farinha and Félix 2015; Cenni et al. 2015 and Ferri et al. 2016), our cross-country dataset allows us to evaluate international differences on the determinants of SMEs financial constraints. Secondly, despite the anecdotal evidence of strong difficulties for small and opaque firms to access to finance, the empirical evidence on the extent of credit rationing due to asymmetric information is scarce. In our contribution, we introduce a proxy of the asymmetric information through the variable R&D. As well known, information asymmetries justify higher R&D self-financing rates compared to traditional investment rates suggesting more difficulties for innovative firms in the access to bank loans (Hall 2002). Thirdly, we introduce hard and soft information in the attempt to explain the supply side reasons of credit rationing.

Our main findings reveal that distinct demand and supply side factors determine credit rationing and heterogeneous results emerge for the different countries. As for weak rationing—defined as the condition for which a firm asking for more credit at the same interest rate did not receive it—being strongly bank dependent implies a greater probability to be credit rationed; differently solid accounting data, collateral, and greater size may loosen such a condition in crisis times. However, bank relationship-lending attitude as well as larger size may weaken the condition for which a firm, even if ready to accept worse interest rates, did not receive credit, i.e., strong credit rationing; different to offer, collateral as well as R&D propensity may strengthen it because of moral hazard risk and higher information asymmetries.

The chapter is organized as follows. Section 4.2 reviews the literature on credit rationing with respect to SMEs. Sections 4.3 and 4.4 present data and methodology. Section 4.5 describes the results. Section 4.6 offers some concluding remarks.

## 4.2 Demand and Supply Side Credit Determinants Literature Review

The traditional literature on financial intermediation (Leland and Pyle 1977; Diamond 1984; Thakor 1995) suggests that credit markets are imperfect because of the asymmetric information between the lender and the borrower. According to Berger and Udell (1998), the firm capital structure varies with asymmetric information along with the firm financial growth cycle. In this respect, small, young, and innovative firms appear more informatively opaque, and for this reason, they may be more credit rationed than other more transparent firms. According to the theory, credit rationing comes in two forms. Borrower rationing (type 1) means that some borrowers get no loan at all, although they may have profitable investment projects and are indistinguishable from those borrowers who receive loans (Stiglitz and Weiss 1981). Loan size rationing (type 2) means that, at the current interest rate, all borrowers are served but demand a larger loan amount than they finally receive from the bank (Jaffee and Russell 1976).

According to the literature, some solutions to the above credit market disequilibrium come from: (i) a long and repeated relationship between the lender and the borrower, i.e., relationship lending (Petersen and Rajan 1994; Cole 1998; Boot 2000; etc.); (ii) the ability to provide signals through self-financing, collateral, etc. (Leland and Pyle 1977; Bester 1985)[1].

Despite the importance of the topic from a theoretical point of view, it is difficult to produce empirical evidence due to a lack of micro-level demand and supply data. Nevertheless, it is possible to disentangle the demand and supply side determinants of credit rationing by exploiting different types of dataset and identifying alternative strategies of investigation. First, the recent literature investigates the credit supply during the current crisis. Using credit registry data on bank–firm relationships in Italy after Lehman's collapse, Albertazzi and Marchetti (2010) produce evidence of a contraction of credit supply driven by larger less capitalized banks. Similar results emerge for Spain for which Jiménez et al. (2012) confirm that a restrictive monetary policy produces more severe credit-rationing effects for banks with low capital or liquidity. Following a similar approach, Iyer et al. (2014) show for Portugal that the credit supply reduction is stronger in the case of smaller and weakly banking relationship firms. Using a partial dataset including detailed balance-sheet information on the universe of Portuguese SMEs, Farinha and Félix (2015) disentangle supply side credit-rationing factors finding similar results.

Other papers apply a disequilibrium model in the attempt to identify credit-constrained firms. In this respect, Kremp and Sevestre (2013) combine information from individual company database and the financial linkage database available at the Bank of France, and after having separated demand and supply-driven credit factors find that French SMEs do not appear to be strongly credit rationed since 2008. Following a similar approach, Carbo-Valverde et al. (2012) find a significant evidence of a general credit crunch in the SME sector during the crisis. However, distinguishing between two alternative sources of finance and between credit-constrained and unconstrained SMEs imply interesting results: (i) constrained SMEs depend on trade credit, but not on bank loans to finance their investments during the crisis; (ii) unconstrained SMEs are dependent on bank loans not on trade credit. In other terms, trade credit may be a good bank credit substitute during the financial crisis.

Finally, other studies aim to identify constrained firms using survey data containing information on loan applications and bank decisions. By exploiting a survey on Italian manufacturing firms, interviewed from March 2008 to February 2010 by the Institute of Studies and Economic Analysis (ISAE), Presbitero et al. (2014) find evidence that there was a significant contraction of credit in Italy in the post-Lehman period. Their main results suggest that credit rationing has been more severe in the area characterized by a high concentration of branches owned by distantly managed banks. Moreover, evidence suggests that small and opaque firms have not been credit rationed more severely than larger ones, contradicting the common idea of a flight to quality by banks and especially by nationwide banks. This result is in line with the literature on bank–firm distance (Alessandrini et al. 2009). As the bank–firm distance increases, it becomes more difficult to evaluate the borrower quality. In this respect, firms located in functionally distant credit markets even if large and transparent are more credit rationed than firms located in credit markets largely populated by functionally closer banks (Presbitero et al. 2014).

Based on a two-wave survey jointly conducted by the World Bank and the European Bank for Reconstruction and Development over the periods 2005 and 2008, Popov and Udell (2012) identify a sample of firms operating in 16 European emerging countries. Their main results suggest that credit rationing depends on supply side factors and is more severe when banks are under-capitalized, and depends also on demand factors being the credit restraint greater for riskier and less transparent firms.

As for Europe, the Directorate General Research of the European Commission supported another survey (i.e., the EFIGE survey), the same used in this chapter, with the aim to collect qualitative information about firm–bank relationship and firm access to credit for a comprehensive sample of companies operating in seven European countries (Germany, France, Italy, Spain, the United Kingdom, Austria, and Hungary). Based on this dataset, some papers investigate the credit-rationing conditions and their effects in terms of international activities and R&D. Aristei and Franco (2014), for example, find that exporters and high productivity firms are less likely to be credit constrained. Mancusi and Vezzulli (2014) show that credit rationing negatively affects both the probability to set up R&D activities and the level of R&D spending (conditioned on the R&D decision). Moreover, Altomonte et al. (2016) find no significant relationship between investing in R&D and the probability to be credit constrained, conditional on exporting. This suggests that efficiency-improving strategies, mediated by the existence of credit constraints, are at the core of firm growth achieved through exporting and innovation. Finally, more recently Ferri et al. (2016) investigate the relationship between bank lending technologies and the credit rationing. Their main results suggest that "the use of transaction lending technologies generally worsened credit rationing [...]. On the contrary, the use of relational lending technologies heightened credit rationing in no specification" (p. 7).

Different from the previous contributions, in the rest of the chapter, we try to disentangle demand (e.g., self-financing, investment decision and collateral) and supply side factors (e.g., credit scoring and relationship-lending variables) of credit rationing. Particularly attention is given to the role of both collateral and R&D on credit rationing.

Following the firm growth life cycle à la Berger and Udell (1998), we expect that R&D activities may increase the risk of credit rationing, the contrary holds in the case of collateralized assets.

## 4.3   Data

Our empirical analysis relies on survey-based information about firm–bank relationship and firm access to credit for a comprehensive sample of European companies, the EU-EFIGE/BRUEGEL-UNICREDIT

DATASET (in short the EFIGE dataset), a database recently collected within the EFIGE project (European Firms in a Global Economy: internal policies for external competitiveness) supported by the Directorate General Research of the European Commission.

The database, for the first time in Europe, combines measures of firms' international activities (e.g., exports, outsourcing, FDI, imports) with quantitative and qualitative information on about 150 items ranging from R&D and innovation, labor organization, financing and organizational activities, and pricing behavior. Data consist of a representative sample (at the country level for the manufacturing industry) of almost 15,000 surveyed firms (above 10 employees) in seven European economies (Germany, France, Italy, Spain, the United Kingdom, Austria, and Hungary). Data were carried out in 2010; it covers the years from 2007 to 2009. Special questions related to the behavior of firms during the crisis were also included in the survey. The survey data are coupled with complete firms financial accounting data from Amadeus–Bureau Van Dijk for each fiscal year from 2006 to 2009.

### 4.3.1 Demand and Credit-Rationing Definitions

The survey provides detailed cross-sectional information on firms' financial constraints, based on firms' responses to the following questions: (i) "During the last year, was the firm willing to increase its borrowing at the same interest rate" (question F13); (ii) "During the last year, did the firm apply for more credit?" (question F14) and (iii) "To increase its borrowing, would the firm have been prepared to pay a higher rate of interest?" (question F15).

Different from previous papers using this dataset or similar datasets (see, among others, Minetti and Zhu 2011; Aristei and Franco 2014; Cenni et al. 2015), we first distinguish between credit demand factors and credit supply factors. Indeed, the above question (F13) underlines the firm availability to ask for credit. The CREDIT_DEMAND variable assumes the value of 1 if the answer to the above question is yes and 0 otherwise.

It is only by introducing supply factors that we can refer to a WEAK_RATIONING variable by which the rationed firms are those

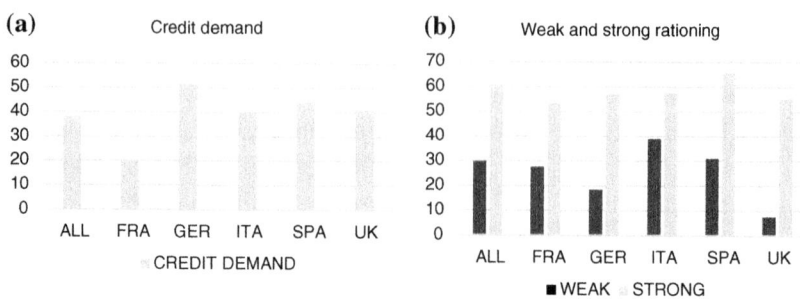

**Fig. 4.1** Distribution of credit demand, weakly and strongly rationed firms

that replied "Yes" to the first question (F13) and "Yes, applied for it but was not successful" to the second one (F14). The variable assumes the value of 1 if it was not successful and 0 otherwise.

We also consider a further measure of STRONG_RATIONING identifying as strongly financially constrained those firms willing to increase their borrowing paying a higher interest rate without being successful (F15). The variable assumes the value of 1 if the answer to the above question is yes and 0 otherwise (in this last case, the firm is weakly but not strongly rationed).

Figure 4.1 presents the distribution of credit demand, weakly and strongly rationed firms based on the above definitions. In the whole sample, among those firms asking for credit, 38% of the entire sample (panel a), those weakly rationed are 30%, while those strongly rationed are 61% (panel b). When we disaggregate the analysis by country, we note significant heterogeneities: Italy and Spain display the highest rate of firms being weakly financially constrained firms (37% and 31%, respectively) because tightening in credit availability during the crisis. The UK is characterized by the lowest proportion of weakly rationed firms (7%) followed by Germany (18%) and France (27%). Quite homogenous patterns emerge for those firms that being ready to pay a higher interest rate to obtain credit have nonetheless been rationed suggesting banks have correctly previously selected their borrowers. The UK and Germany stand as the countries with the highest percentage difference between weakly and strongly rationed firms (48% and 39%, respectively). These results suggest that, in these countries, intermediaries have only partially reduced access to credit by denying applications, but tightened lending conditions (i.e., higher interest rates and tougher collateral requirements) may have increased the cost of credit and discouraged firms from applying.

## 4.3.2 Credit Demand Factors

According to the previous literature (see, among the others, Kremp and Sevestre 2013; Farinha and Félix 2015), we assume that the demand for new loans depends on the following factors:

- the financing needs. To evaluate financing needs, we introduce a variable based on the following two questions: "During 2009 has your firm reduced its planned investments in machinery, equipment or ICT?" (question C13A). The answer could be either Yes or No. The next question asked for the percentage, in the range 1–100, in the reduction in planned investments in machinery, equipment, or ICT (question C13APERC). The investments' dynamic comes from the combination of two questions and signals the extent to which the firm reduced its planned investments in machinery, equipment, or ICT during 2009. This variable is identified as RED_INV;
- the size of the firm; smaller firms are indeed expected to rely more on bank loans than larger ones which may have an easier access to other external forms of financing. In line with the prevalent literature, we proxy the size of the firm in terms of log total asset, SIZE. To control for potential nonlinear effect, we introduce also the square of the size variable, SIZE_SQR;
- the amount of internal resources. We follow previous papers and measure internal resources by the firm's EBITDA over its total assets. We name this variable SELF_FIN;
- the age of the firm is proxied by a categorical variable for the year of establishment (<6 years; 6–20 years; >20 years), the first class, AGE identifies young companies (question A1);
- the amount of other sources of external finance available. These are taken into account through the variable Credit dependency that is

derived from the following demand: "In the industry your firm works, how dependent are companies on external financing?" (question F4). The reply stands in the range 1–5 where "1 = not dependent at all" and "5 = extremely dependent" and the variable is labeled as CRED_DEP;

- the cost of borrowing. In literature, the cost of borrowing is proxied by different measures. For instance, Carbo-Valverde et al. (Carbo-Valverde et al. 2012) use the spread with an interbank rate, while Shikimi (2005) uses the difference with a prime rate. Ogawa and Kitasaka (2000) and Atanasova and Wilson (2004) account for interest rates by a set of year dummies. In our contribution, the cost of borrowing is directly inferred by the demand "With reference to the last year has your firm experienced an increase of the cost of debt charged?" (question F18) and is labeled CREDIT_COST;
- the degree of innovation is captured by the percentage of the total turnover the firm invest in R&D. The variable, named RD_PERC, is a dummy linked to the answer to the following question (question C21): Which percentage of the total turnover has the firm invested in R&D on average in the last 3 years (2007–2009)?

### 4.3.3 Credit-Rationing Factors

As for the credit rationing, we assume that supply factors depend on two main set of variables based on the literature on bank–firm relationship (see, among others, Berger and Udell 2006; and more recently Udell 2015): (i) the relationship banking variables; and (ii) the firm's characteristics variables.

As suggested by the literature, a continuous and repeated relationship between the bank and the borrower, i.e., a relationship-lending condition, can loosen the information asymmetry problems. This is particularly true for SMEs. In the main empirical literature, the variables most used to proxy the bank–firm relationship are based on the information that a bank can accumulate on the borrower's history (see, e.g., Petersen and Rajan 1994; Berger and Udell 1995). To measure this attitude, a set of variables are introduced: (i) MAIN_BANK; (ii) MULTI_BANK; (iii) DURATION; (iv) LOCAL_BANK.

The importance of the MAIN_BANK for the firm is captured by the question (F10) "What % of your firm's total bank debt is held at your main bank?" The percentage that gives evidence of the main bank debt share stands in the range between 1 and 100% and is transformed in log terms.

The MULTI_BANK variable measures the presence of multiple banking relationships and is captured by the question (F9) "Number of banks." The number stands in the range between 1 and 99 and is transformed in log terms.

The length of the relationship with the main bank, DURATION, is captured by the demand (F11) "For how many years has this bank been the firm's main bank?" The number stands in the range between 1 and 99 and is transformed in log terms.

The proximity between bank and firm, LOCAL_BANK is captured by two demands (F8A and F8B) that enable to understand whether domestic or foreign activities are accrued out with domestic local banks. The variables are dichotomous.

As the bank decision to grant credit depends to some extent on hard information (Berger and Udell 2006), we insert in the model the company's financial situation proxied by the Z_SCORE variable. Here, we use one of the principal measures of companies' financial distress probability, that is, the version of the Z-Score model developed by Altman (1983) for private non-US corporates suitable for manufacturing and non-manufacturing firms (the so-called Z''-Score [EM] model). Each company was given a score (Z''-Score [EM]) composed of a discriminant function of four variables weighted by coefficients. Analytically, the Z''-Score [EM] (Altman et al. 1995) is estimated as:

$$Z'' - \text{Score [EM]} = +3.25 + 6.56 X_1 + 3.26 X_2 + 6.72 X_3 + 1.05 X_4$$

$$(4.1)$$

where the first ratio, Working capital/Total assets ($X1$), is a measure of the net liquid assets of the firm relative to total assets; $X2$ is a measure of cumulative profitability and refers to the earned surplus of a firm over its entire life; the EBIT/Total assets ratio ($X3$) is a measure of the true productivity or profitability of the assets of a firm, not affected by any tax or leverage factors; and X4 shows how much the firm's assets can decline in value (measured by book value of equity plus debt) before the liabilities exceed the assets and the firm becomes insolvent. This model measures the probability that a company will enter bankruptcy within a 12-month period; in other words, it measures the firm's financial health. Higher Z″-Score [EM] values indicate lower risk of financial distress. Of the different versions of the Z-Score model developed by Altman, we chose the Z″-Score [EM] for several reasons. First in the sample, very few firms are public; moreover, it has been shown that the Z″-Score model applied to non-US companies is far more robust than the other models (Altman and Hotchkiss 2006). Last but not least, several contributions[2] show that the original coefficients are extremely robust across countries and over time.

The other variable that has been shown to play an important role in banks' lending decisions is the firm ability to provide COLLATERAL. In line with Carbo-Valverde et al. (2009) and Kremp and Sevestre (2013), we use the ratio of tangible assets to total assets to account for the firm available collateral.

Finally, the SIZE variable can reflect both the likelihood to go bankrupt (smaller firms are more likely to do so than larger ones) and the level of collateral that can be provided by firms as a guarantee for their loan. Indeed, it is well known (Berger and Udell 1998) that younger firms characterized in particular by a high degree of innovation are more likely to default than mature ones (e.g., see Fougère et al. 2012). In this respect, Fig. 4.2 presents the distribution of firms by credit rationing

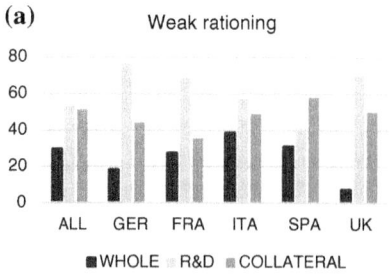
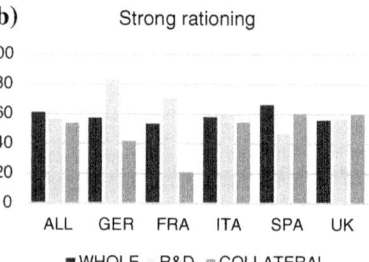

**Fig. 4.2** R&D, collateral and credit rationing

**Table 4.1** Summary statistics for the full sample

| Variable | Description | Obs | Mean | Std. Dev. | Min | Max |
|---|---|---|---|---|---|---|
| | | All | | | | |
| CREDIT_DEMAND | Question F13: Would the firm have used more credit at the same interest rate? = 1 if yes; = 0 otherwise | 6,301 | 0.390 | 0.488 | 0.000 | 1.000 |
| WEAK_RATIONING | Question F14: Did the firm applied for more credit? = 0 if received; = 1 if denied | 1,904 | 0.702 | 0.457 | 0.000 | 1.000 |
| STRONG_RATIONING | Question F15: Would the firm have paid a higher interest rate to receive credit? 1 if yes; = 0 otherwise | 565 | 0.607 | 0.489 | 0.000 | 1.000 |
| MAIN_BANK | Question F10: Main bank share of credit | 6,471 | 3.745 | 1.092 | 0.000 | 4.615 |
| MULTI_BANK | Question F9: Number of banks used | 13,733 | 0.932 | 0.643 | 0.000 | 4.595 |
| DURATION | Question F11: Years with the main bank | 6,361 | 2.440 | 0.887 | 0.000 | 4.595 |
| LOCAL_BANK | Question F8: Does the firm use a local bank? = 1 if yes = 0 otherwise | 10,597 | 0.963 | 0.820 | 0.000 | 2.000 |
| Z_SCORE | Altman Z-Score_2008 | 8,645 | 5.600 | 7.743 | −517.510 | 75.774 |
| COLLATERAL | Tangible_TA = (tangible fixed assets 2008/total assets 2008) | 12,234 | 0.254 | 0.200 | 0.000 | 0.989 |
| CREDIT_DEP | Question F3: Dependency from Credit of the company's sector: categorical 1 (not at all)—5 (extremely) | 13,465 | 2.851 | 1.300 | 1.000 | 5.000 |
| SIZE | Ln (total assets2007 + total assets 2008 + total assets 2009)/3 | 10,786 | 7.942 | 1.406 | 1.439 | 16.130 |
| SIZE_SQR | (SIZE)^2 | 10,786 | 65.053 | 23.973 | 0.076 | 260.193 |
| AGE | Categorical variable: = 1 if firm 1–5 years | 13,828 | 0.069 | 0.254 | 0.000 | 1.000 |

(continued)

**Table 4.1** (continued)

| Variable | Description | Obs | Mean | Std. Dev. | Min | Max |
|---|---|---|---|---|---|---|
| | | All | | | | |
| | = 2 if firm 6–20 years | 13,828 | 0.338 | 0.473 | 0.000 | 1.000 |
| | = 3 if firm > 20 years | 13,828 | 0.592 | 0.491 | 0.000 | 1.000 |
| RD_PERC | Question C21: Which percentage of the total turnover has the firm invested in R&D on average in the last three years (2007–2009)? | 13,821 | 3.664 | 7.707 | 0.000 | 100.000 |
| RED_INV | Question: C13A: Reduction in planned investments in machinery, equipment or ICT | 11,709 | 24.200 | 36.158 | 0.000 | 100.000 |
| SELF_FIN | Ebitda 2009/Total Assets 2009 | 8,660 | −0.090 | 13.111 | −1,219.945 | 2.582 |
| CREDIT_COST | Question F18: With reference to the last year has your firm experienced an increase in the cost of debt charged? | 6,433 | 0.442 | 0.497 | 0.000 | 1.000 |

and the above firm characteristics. The literature suggests that small and young firms may suffer financial constraints because of information asymmetries that increase in the case of R&D activity. Therefore, rationing probability may increase. As for our sample, the probability of weak and strong rationing for very young firms (less than 6 years) and for very small firms (less than 10 million of total assets) is nearly 90% confirming the underlying theory. As for the R&D propensity, measured by the RD_PERC variable, our results suggest that in all countries, the probability to be weakly rationed increased in the case of innovative firms. A similar pattern emerges in case of strong credit rationing for all countries except for Spain where innovative firms do not appear to be more strongly rationed. As for the COLLATERAL, our results suggest that, contrary to the idea that tangible assets may increase the bank creditworthiness in the firm, a moral hazard effect dominates, and consequently, the more collateralized the firm is, the more it is credit rationed. This is particularly true for Italy and Spain. However, in France and Germany, the collateral may mitigate the strong rationing effect compared to the weak one. All variable details—description and descriptive statistics for the full sample—are reported in Table 4.1.

## 4.4 Methodology

To investigate how demand factors influence the CREDIT_DEMAND, i.e., a dichotomy variable assuming value 0 if the firm was not willing to increase its borrowing at the same interest rate and 1 otherwise (Question F13 of the EFIGE questionnaire), we follow a standard logit scheme.

From an empirical point view, we estimate the following Eq. (4.2):

$$\text{CREDIT DEMAND} =$$
$$\alpha_0 + \beta_{1-4}(\text{Demand Factors}) + \gamma_{1-5}(\text{Controls}) + \delta_{1-4}(\text{Country Dummy}) + \varepsilon \quad (4.2)$$

The vector of explanatory variables X includes both demand variables (RED_INV, SELF_FIN, and CREDIT_COST), controls (AGE, SIZE, SIZE_SQR, RD_PERC, and CREDIT_DEP) and country dummy only in the case of the full sample.

As a second step, we analyze the reasons of WEAK_RATIONING. We define a firm as weakly credit rationed if it asked more credit (answered yes to Question F13, i.e., CREDIT_DEMAND $= 1$) and, conditional to this, it applied for more credit but was denied by the banks (answered YES, applied for credit but was not successful to Question F14, i.e., WEAK_RATIONING $= 0$). We observe WEAK_RATIONING $= 0$ if and only if CREDIT_DEMAND $= 1$. In other terms, the probability of being rationed depends on the probability the firm decides to ask for credit. To tackle this type of problem, known in the literature as sample selection problem, we employ a bivariate Probit model with selection, i.e., a variant of the Heckman Selection Model (1979).[3] The model is based on two equations: (a) a selection equation in which we model the probability that the firm ask for more credit (CD); (b) an outcome equation in which we model the probability of being rationed (WR), which is the censored sample since it is possible to observe the outcome if and only if at the first step a positive selection has been done.

The empirical specification of the above CD and WR equations is as follows:

$$
\begin{aligned}
WR^* = &\alpha_0 + \mu_{1-4}(\text{Relationship Lending}) + \tau_{1-2}(\text{Firm characteristics}) + \\
&\gamma_{1-6}^{WR}(\text{Controls}) + \delta_{1-4}^{WR}(\text{Country Dummy}) + u
\end{aligned} \tag{4.3}
$$

$$
\begin{aligned}
CD^* = &\alpha_0 + \beta_{1-4}(\text{Demand Factors}) + \gamma_{1-5}^{CD}(\text{Controls}) \\
&+ \delta_{1-4}^{CD}(\text{Country Dummy}) + v
\end{aligned} \tag{4.4}
$$

As for the selection equation (Eq. 4.3), the explanatory variables include demand factors, i.e., RED_INV, SELF_FIN, and CREDIT_COST, and controls include SIZE, SIZE_SQR, AGE, and RD_PERC and country dummy only in the case of the full sample. In the outcome equation (Eq. 4.4), relationship-lending variables include MAIN_BANK, MULTI_BANK, DURATION, and LOCAL_BANK; firm characteristics include, respectively, Z_SCORE and COLLATERAL; controls include AGE, SIZE, SIZE_SQR, and RD_PERC and the industry credit dependency condition, i.e., CREDIT_DEP, while the country dummy includes the same variables as the selection equation.

Finally, we analyze the reasons of STRONG_RATIONING. We define a firm as strongly credit rationed if among those firms being weakly rationed (applying for more credit and being denied), they would have been available to pay a higher interest rate to obtain more credit (answered YES, to the question F15, i.e., STRONG_RATIONING $= 1$). As for the credit demand variable, the strong rationing is a dichotomy variable assuming value 0 if the firm was not willing to increase its borrowing at a higher interest rate and 1 otherwise and the estimates models are based on a standard logit scheme. From an empirical point view, we estimate the following equation:

$$STRONG\,RATIONING =$$
$$\alpha_0 + \beta_{1-4}(Relationship\,lending) + \mu_{1-2}(Firm\,characteristics) + \gamma_{1-5}(Controls)+$$
$$\delta_{1-4}(Country\,Dummy) + \varepsilon \qquad (4.5)$$

where here the controls as in the Eq. (4.3) include only SIZE, SIZE_SQR, AGE, and RD_PERC. It is important to note that question F15 of the questionnaire is not self-selection with respect to F14 being considering only denied customers. In this sense, we do not apply a Heckman procedure but we are going to estimate the alternatives to the question "To increase its borrowing, would the firm have been prepared to pay a higher rate of interest?" (F15), $1 =$ Yes and 0 otherwise.

## 4.5   Results

Tables 4.2, 4.3, and 4.4 report the results of our econometric analysis. First, we discuss the results from a demand-side point of view (Table 4.2), and then, those more typically linked to the supply side first in a weakly version of credit rationing (Table 4.3) and then in a strongly credit-rationing condition.

As for the demand side (Table 4.2), the main results suggest heterogeneous patterns among the European countries here considered. First, a liquidity problem appears more evident for countries such as Italy and Spain. The credit demand increases as the firm investments, RED_INV follow a declining trend because of the current crisis. This counterintuitive result suggests that even if the investment slackened, firms

Table 4.2  The demand side

| Variable | All | Italy | Spain | Germany | France | The UK |
|---|---|---|---|---|---|---|
| RED_INV | 0.00059** | 0.00141*** | 0.00053* | 0.00024 | −0.00042 | −0.00122 |
| | (0.00020) | (0.00036) | (0.00033) | (0.00166) | (0.00035) | (0.00131) |
| SELF_FIN | −0.13256* | −0.60711** | −0.21187* | −0.35878 | −0.06368 | 0.45239 |
| | (0.06787) | (0.30074) | (0.10919) | (0.33812) | (0.09358) | (0.36979) |
| AGE | 0.07559** | 0.10947** | 0.13629** | −0.16112 | −0.01258 | −0.14361 |
| | (0.03032) | (0.04840) | (0.05631) | (0.16057) | (0.06320) | (0.18117) |
| SIZE | 0.03729 | 0.01523 | 0.08986 | −0.02468 | −0.02194 | 0.10911 |
| | (0.04458) | (0.08556) | (0.07461) | (0.42492) | (0.07089) | (0.18311) |
| SIZE_SQR | −0.0017 | −0.00088 | −0.00391 | −0.00052 | 0.00157 | −0.00621 |
| | (0.00247) | (0.00455) | (0.00428) | (0.02292) | (0.00393) | (0.01032) |
| CREDIT_DEP | 0.05069*** | 0.07796*** | 0.03253** | −0.00275 | 0.03129** | 0.04301 |
| | (0.00670) | (0.01110) | (0.01110) | (0.04073) | (0.01233) | (0.03251) |
| CREDIT_COST | 0.18863*** | 0.19704*** | 0.26601*** | 0.08336 | 0.11443*** | −0.19949** |
| | (0.01432) | (0.02332) | (0.02260) | (0.09224) | (0.03035) | (0.07416) |
| RD_PERC | 0.00116 | 0.00221 | 0.00224 | −0.01908** | 0.00132 | −0.00065 |
| | (0.00106) | (0.00160) | (0.00209) | (0.00958) | (0.00161) | (0.00613) |
| DUMMY_FR | −0.28368*** | | | | | |
| | (0.04580) | | | | | |
| DUMMY_SP | −0.09267** | | | | | |
| | (0.04322) | | | | | |
| DUMMY_IT | −0.08472* | | | | | |
| | (0.04355) | | | | | |
| DUMMY_UK | −0.13094** | | | | | |
| | (0.05866) | | | | | |
| N. obs | 3,643 | 1,334 | 1,272 | 127 | 763 | 147 |
| Wald $\chi^2(12)$ | 360.96*** | 176.1*** | 140.37*** | 6.58 | 28.03** | 12.61 |
| Pseudo-$R^2$ | 0.0916 | 0.1165 | 0.0894 | 0.0517 | 0.0363 | 0.0746 |
| Log-pseudolikelihood | −2174.2355 | −780.94944 | −793.45312 | −83.293415 | −365.79013 | −91.631352 |

***, **, and * indicate statistical significance at the 1%, 5%, and 10% level, respectively. Regression coefficients are reported with standard error in parenthesis

For a description of the variables, see Table 4.1

**Table 4.3** The weak credit rationing

| Variable | All | Italy | Spain |
|---|---|---|---|
| Outcome | | | |
| MAIN_BANK | 0.05753 | 0.05619 | 0.0301 |
| | (0.05649) | (0.10522) | (0.13207) |
| MULTI_BANK | 0.05896 | 0.11501 | 0.06417 |
| | (0.08729) | (0.14561) | (0.22098) |
| DURATION | 0.08042* | 0.0419 | 0.06899 |
| | (0.04532) | (0.07765) | (0.08335) |
| LOCAL_BANK | 0.01414 | 0.01264 | −0.04155 |
| | (0.04785) | (0.0811) | (0.08819) |
| Z_SCORE | 0.04413** | 0.08134** | 0.05893 |
| | (0.01950) | (0.03209) | (0.06666) |
| COLLATERAL | 0.29042 | 0.97226** | 0.16193 |
| | (0.21949) | (0.39017) | (0.35492) |
| CREDIT_DEP | −0.14978*** | −0.16761** | −0.09451* |
| | (0.04016) | (0.06975) | (0.06008) |
| SIZE | 0.72430** | −0.63406 | 0.68126* |
| | (0.30053) | (0.78910) | (0.40522) |
| SIZE_SQR | −0.03578** | 0.02884 | −0.02974 |
| | (0.01630) | (0.04071) | (0.02327) |
| AGE | 0.08419 | 0.21909 | −0.23900 |
| | (0.1872) | (0.29275) | (0.30163) |
| RD_PERC | 0.00178 | −0.00229 | 0.01777* |
| | (0.00567) | (0.008599) | (0.01008) |
| DUMMY_FR | −0.03497 | | |
| | (0.23773) | | |
| DUMMY_SP | −0.15958 | | |
| | (0.22783) | | |
| DUMMY_IT | 0.36606* | | |
| | (0.24353) | | |
| DUMMY_UK | −0.26416 | | |
| | (0.35325) | | |
| Cons | −3.64341** | 2.85559 | −3.43342* |
| | (1.47208) | (3.75531) | (1.83030) |

asked for more credit, probably because of other reasons, mainly liquidity reasons. The sign of SELF_FIN corroborates this result. As the internal financial sources increase, the firm prefers to reduce the demand of external more expensive financial sources, e.g., the bank credit (Myers and Majluf 1984)[4]. A common pattern holds for Italy and Spain in the case of AGE. The younger the SMEs are, the higher the probability

**Table 4.4** The strong credit rationing

| Variable | All | Italy | Spain |
|---|---|---|---|
| MAIN_BANK | 0.0089 | 0.0712 | 0.00156 |
| | (0.03436) | (0.06438) | (0.04176) |
| MULTI_BANK | 0.20981*** | 0.34748*** | 0.11225 |
| | (0.05613) | (0.08645) | (0.10425) |
| DURATION | −0.03013 | −0.01591 | −0.01741 |
| | (0.03408) | (0.05135) | (0.05753) |
| LOCAL_BANK | −0.01087 | 0.06483 | −0.04624 |
| | (0.03273) | (0.04638) | (0.04685) |
| COLLATERAL | 0.08320 | 0.35956* | −0.25859 |
| | (0.13899) | (0.20193) | (0.21461) |
| SIZE | −0.31994* | −0.7410659* | −0.10819 |
| | (0.21466) | (0.46767) | (0.16992) |
| SIZE_SQR | 0.0174 | 0.0383943* | 0.00771 |
| | (0.01248) | (0.02614) | (0.01153) |
| AGE | −0.00621 | 0.03101 | −0.07878 |
| | (0.10333) | (0.15113) | (0.14717) |
| RD_PERC | 0.00883** | 0.00707* | 0.04598*** |
| | (0.00386) | (0.00386) | (0.01274) |
| N. obs | 297 | 141 | 108 |
| Wald $\chi^2(9)$ | 20.45** | 20.81** | 19.98** |
| Pseudo-$R^2$ | 0.0609 | 0.1047 | 0.1421 |
| Log-pseudolikelihood | −186.1694 | −86.35185 | −57.02945 |

***, **, and * indicate statistical significance at the 1%, 5%, and 10% level, respectively. Regression coefficients are reported with standard error in parenthesis

For a description of the variables, see Table 4.1

they ask for more credit. At the first stage of their life, SMEs have low internal sources of finance and in countries such as Italy and Spain typically bank oriented, the main source of external finance is bank credit (Berger and Udell 1998). The result is further reinforced by the sign of CREDIT_DEP that holds also for France and suggests that as a firm holding to an industry sector is strongly dependent on the banking system, the probability to ask for more credit increases. Differently, as an obvious consequence from the theory (Rajan 1992), more market-oriented countries have more opportunities to ask for other types of external financing sources. This opportunity is confirmed in the case of the UK, the only country for which as the CREDIT_COST increases, the probability of asking for credit decreases. The contrary holds for those countries such as Italy, Spain, and France characterized by a bank-oriented financial system. The fact that the firms in the UK are more market oriented and use external finance sources other than bank loans is confirmed by the fact that if the credit cost increases bank loans demand decreases. The contrary hold for the firms from other countries given that for them the access to market external finance sources is more difficult.

Among the traditional bank-oriented financial countries, Germany represents at least partially an exception. In fact, as the R&D propensity increases, i.e., the asymmetric information between the bank and the borrower increases, the firm demands for credit decreases suggesting the opportunity for German innovative firms to access to alternative source of finance. The same conclusion may hold for the UK where the R&D variable is not statistically significant probably because of an ex ante self-selection problem, i.e., firms more R&D oriented are out of this sample.

Finally, the analysis of the country dummies suggests some heterogeneity among the countries of our sample. Results suggest that Italian, French, Spanish, and UK firms ask for less credit than the German ones.

Combining supply and demand side factors Table 4.3 shows results on the determinants of the weak rationing both in the selection equation identifying the CREDIT_DEMAND determinants and then in the outcome equation identifying the WEAK_RATIONING determinants. We present the results for the full sample and for Italy and Spain. The limited number of observations does not permit the same exercise for the other countries. As Italy and Spain present similar country characteristics, this exercise appears quite interesting from an economic point of view.

The decision for asking or not credit—*selection equation*—depends on demand factors, i.e., the investment decision INV_RED, the cost of credit CREDIT_COST as well as on firm structural characteristics like the size of the firm, SIZE. As in the analysis on the credit demand, a reduction in the firm investment as well as an increase in the cost of credit implies more credit demand suggesting a strong dependency of the firm on the credit channel. This result holds for the full sample and partly for Italy where, even if the CREDIT_COST variable is not statistically significant, the negative sign of SELF_FIN confirms that the liquidity problems drives the credit demand during the crisis.

The economic literature suggests that, usually, the smaller the SMEs are, the greater the information asymmetries with the potential lender so that they suffer potential credit-rationing problems more strongly than larger firms do. The reason relates to the fact that information about economic and financial small firms' performances is less accessible than for larger ones (Diamond and Verrecchia 1991; Kremp and Sevestre 2013; Cenni et al. 2015). As for our results, the evidence suggests that the higher the firm size, the greater the credit demand; moreover, the smaller the firm, the more severe the credit-rationing problem.

As for the R&D, our results are partly in contradiction with respect to previous literature (Mancusi and Vezzulli 2014). As RD_PERC increases, the weak rationing decreases. However, this result appears to be statistically significant only for Spain where the existence of some particular incentives could justify the result.

The literature on credit rationing emphasizes the role of relationship-lending variables as a way to reduce the information asymmetries between the bank and the lender (Sette and Gobbi 2015). As for our sample, these variables do not play any important role being statistical significantly only the DURATION for the full sample. As the duration between the firm and the lender increases, the credit rationing decreases. That relationship lending plays a role in defining the risk of credit rationing emerges from the analysis of the CREDIT_DEP variable. A firm belonging to a sector strongly dependent on bank credit may emphasize the bank soft-budget constraint risk. In this sense, as a firm is highly bank dependent, the more is the risk of being credit rationed.

The more recent literature (Brighi et al. 2016) underlines the complementary role of soft and hard information in defining credit risk. In this sense, credit rationing depends also on accounting firm variables as well as on their collateral. Our results confirm that as Z_SCORE and COLLATERAL increase, the firm is safer and the credit rationing decreases.

As for the country dummies contrary to the simple demand analysis, the Heckman selection model suggests that at the outcome step,

Italy asks for more credit than Germany; the contrary holds for the UK. Moreover, at the selection step, i.e., once Italian firms have been selected to be credit worthy they are less credit rationed than the German ones.

As a final exercise, we verify which factors may determine a STRONG RATIONING condition exclusively driven by supply side factors. Table 4.4 summarizes the main results. Among the relationship-lending variables, credit rationing weakens as the number of relations increase. This result is coherent with the evidence that firms strongly dependent on bank credit may be credit threatened (see CRED_DEP effects in Table 4.3). Evidence suggests, in other words, that during crisis time, relationship-lending variables lose their importance in driving credit availability decisions. As for Italy, evidence suggests COLLATERAL negatively affect credit availability.

During crisis time, banks consider the moral hazard risk as the prevailing characteristic of a collateralized loan (Steijvers and Voordeckers 2009). SIZE as suggested by the literature negatively affects credit rationing. In this sense—contrary to the evidence produced in the case of WEAK_RATIONING—as the firm size increases it is considered less risky and can benefit from less severe credit availability conditions. Finally, the firm R&D propensity as suggested in the literature (Scellato and Ughetto 2010) strengthens the STRONG_RATIONING condition.

## 4.6   Conclusions

In this chapter, we focus on the reasons determining credit-rationing conditions for SMEs in some principal European countries during the first years of the crisis (2007–2009). The aim of the chapter is to disentangle the demand and supply-driven reasons of credit rationing. This approach helps to understand whether during a crisis period, the reasons of the disequilibrium in the credit market relate to firms' worse investment conditions or otherwise to a more bank prudent and selective credit policy.

In this respect, our main findings reveal that distinct demand and supply side factors determine credit rationing and heterogeneous results emerge for different countries. As for the demand side, the main results suggest that some countries show an evident liquidity problem during the crisis time. Even though the investment slackened, firms asked for more credit, probably because of liquidity restraint. Small, young, and innovative firms sound to be more credit constrained than firms in countries where the access to alternative sources of finance is easier, i.e., typically market-oriented countries.

Then, when we pass to examine the weak rationing conditions, results suggest that to be bank dependent implies a greater probability to be credit rationed; differently solid accounting data, collateral, and greater size may loosen such a condition in crisis times.

However, exclusively bank relationships as well as larger size may weaken the condition for which a firm even if available to accept worse interest rates did not receive credit, i.e., strong credit rationing; different to offer, collateral as well as R&D propensity may strengthen it because of moral hazard risk and higher information asymmetries.

From a policy perspective, our analysis suggests that different country conditions may hamper bank–firm relationship and this is particularly true in crisis time. Because of different credit-rationing conditions, the literature that supports the conjecture that access to credit enhances economic growth (see, e.g., Levine 2005) implies interesting policy considerations in terms of different country economic growth patterns. The present analysis does not contain considerations that would capture aspects of economic development but it could represent a good point of departure for future development. Moreover, as suggested in the literature R&D investment firms are typically more credit constrained than other firms. In this respect, to find the reasons of the main causes of the credit rationing becomes important in the attempt to drive the post-crisis recovery.

## Notes

1. For a complete review of the literature on relationship banking, see Bongini et al. (2009).
2. For an extensive review of the literature, see Bellovary et al. (2007).
3. A similar approach is used in Piga and Atzeni (2007) and in Cenni et al. (2015).

4. The pecking-order theory (Mayers and Majluf 1984) implies the existence of a financial hierarchy among the sources of finance used by firms due to the information asymmetries between owners and lenders. The severity of the information asymmetry implies costs, which gradually rise in the transition from self-financing to equity. As a result, firms prefer internal to external finance, and there is a preference for debt over equity when it comes from external sources.

**Acknowledgements** The authors wish to thank the Department of Statistics of the University of Bologna and Cristina Bernini for giving the opportunity to use the dataset.

# Appendix

The logit scheme followed to derive the empirical Eq. (4.2) in the text develops along with the following theoretical function:

$$P = F(Z) = \frac{1}{1 + e^{-Z}} = \frac{1}{1 + e^{-(\alpha + \beta X)}} \tag{4.1A}$$

Where $P$ is the probability that $Z$ takes the value 1 and $F$ is the cumulative logistic probability function; $X$ is the set of regressors; and $\alpha$ and $\beta$ are parameters. It can be shown that the regression equation is equal to:

$$\ln \frac{P}{1+P} = Z = \alpha + \beta X. \tag{4.2A}$$

As for the Heckman scheme the outcome equation probability of being denied credit (WR), given that more credit (CD) was needed, is expressed as follows:

$$Prob(WR_i = 1 | CD_i = 1) = Prob(x_i \beta + u_i > 0 | CD_i = 1) \tag{4.3A}$$

Where the selection equation CD appears as follows:

$$CD^* = zy + v, \qquad CD = 1 \quad \text{if} \quad CD^* > 0, \qquad 0 \text{ otherwise} \tag{4.4A}$$

while the outcome equation WR:

$$WR^* = \mathbf{x}\beta + u, \qquad WR = 1 \quad \text{if} \quad WR^* > 0, \qquad 0 \text{ otherwise}$$

(4.5A)

and:

$$\begin{pmatrix} u \\ v \end{pmatrix} | \mathbf{x}, v \sim N\left[\begin{pmatrix} 0 \\ 0 \end{pmatrix}, \begin{pmatrix} 1 & \rho \\ \rho & 1 \end{pmatrix}\right]$$

and $\mathbf{x}$ and $\mathbf{z}$ are the vectors of the explanatory variable for CD and WR, $\beta$ and $\gamma$ the vectors of parameters, and $u$ and $v$ the error terms. CD* and WR* are the index functions for the Probit models. If the correlation $\rho \neq 0$, it means the two equations are correlated; otherwise, they are independent; i.e., selection and outcome may be estimated taking out of the selection process.

The Heckman self-selection procedure here described is based on a maximum-likelihood estimation approach in which the log-likelihood function to maximize is:

$$\begin{aligned} lnL = & \sum_{CD_i=1,\ WR_i=1} ln\Phi_2\left[x_i\beta, z_i\gamma;\ \rho\right] \\ & + \sum_{CD_i=1,\ WR_i=0} ln\Phi_2\left[-x_i\beta, z_i\gamma;\ -\rho\right] + \sum_{CD_i=0} ln\Phi[-z_i\gamma] \end{aligned}$$

(4.6A)

Where $\Phi_2$ is the joint cumulative probability distribution function with $\rho = Corr[u, v]$ and $\Phi(.)$ the cumulative distribution function of a standard normal random. If $\rho = 0$, then the log-likelihood for the probit model with sample selection is equal to the sum of the probit models for CD and WR.

# References

Albertazzi, U., and D.J. Marchetti. 2010. Credit supply, flight to quality and evergreening: An analysis of bank-firm relationships after Lehman. Bank of Italy Temi di Discussione (Working Paper No 756).

Alessandrini, P., A.F. Presbitero, and A. Zazzaro. 2009. Banks, distances and firms' financing constraints. *Review of Finance* 13: 261–307.

Altman, E.I. 1983. *Corporate financial distress*. New York: Wiley Interscience.

Altman, E.I., and E. Hotchkiss. 2006. *Corporate financial distress and bankruptcy*. Hoboken, NJ: Wiley.

Altman, E.I., J. Hartzell, and M. Peck. 1995. *Emerging markets corporate bonds: A scoring system*. New York: Salomon Brothers.

Altomonte, C., S. Gamba, M.L. Mancusi, and A. Vezzulli. 2016. R&D investments, financing constraints, exporting and productivity. *Economics of Innovation and New Technology* 25 (3): 283–303.

Aristei, D., and C. Franco. 2014. The role of credit constraints on firms' exporting and importing activities. *Industrial and Corporate Change*, dtu032.

Atanasova, C., and N. Wilson. 2004. Disequilibrium in the UK corporate loan market. *Journal of Banking & Finance* 28: 595–614.

Bank of Italy. 2010. Annual report.

Bellovary, J., D. Giacomino, and M. Akers. 2007. A review of bankruptcy prediction studies: 1930 to present. *Journal of Financial Education* 33: 1–42.

Berger, A.N., and G.F. Udell. 1995. Relationship lending and lines of credit in small firm finance. *Journal of Business* 68: 351–381.

Berger, A.N., and G.F. Udell. 1998. The economics of small business finance: The roles of private equity and debt markets in the financial growth cycle. *Journal of Banking & Finance* 22 (6): 613–673.

Berger, A.N., and G.F. Udell. 2006. A more complete conceptual framework for SME finance. *Journal of Banking & Finance* 30: 2945–2966.

Bester, H. 1985. Screening vs. Rationing in credit markets with imperfect information. *American Economic Review* 75: 850–855.

Bongini, P., M.L. Di Battista, and L. Nieri. 2009. Relationship banking: Una soluzione antica contro la crisi recente? *Bancaria* 5: 2–20.

Boot, A.W. 2000. Relationship banking: What do we know? *Journal of financial intermediation* 9 (1): 7–25.

Brighi P., C. Lucarelli, and V. Venturelli. 2016. Predictive strength of lending technologies. mimeo.

Carbo-Valverde, S., F. Rodriguez-Fernandez, and G. Udell. 2009. Bank market power and SME financing constraints. *Review of Finance* 13: 309–340.

Carbo-Valverde, S., F. Rodriguez-Fernandez, and G. Udell. 2012. *Trade credit, the financial crisis, and firm access to finance*. Grenada: University of Grenada.

Cenni, S., S. Monferrà, V. Salotti, M. Sangiorgi, and G. Torluccio. 2015. Credit rationing and relationship lending. Does firm size matter? *Journal of Banking & Finance* 53: 249–265.

Cole, R.A. 1998. The importance of relationships to the availability of credit. *Journal of Banking & Finance* 22 (6): 959–977.

Cole, R.A., L.G. Goldberg, and L.J. White. 2004. Cookie cutter vs. character: The micro structure of small business lending by large and small banks. *Journal of Financial and Quantitative Analysis* 39 (02): 227–251.

Diamond, D.W. 1984. Financial intermediation and delegated monitoring. *The Review of Economic Studies* 51 (3): 393–414.

Diamond, D.W., and R.E. Verrecchia. 1991. Disclosure, liquidity, and the cost of capital. *The Journal of Finance* 46 (4): 1325–1359.

Farinha, L., and S. Félix. 2015. Credit rationing for Portuguese SMEs. *Finance Research Letters* 14: 167–177.

Ferri G., P. Murro, and Z. Rotondib. 2016. Bank lending technologies and SME credit rationing in Europe in the 2009 crisis. (CERBE Working Paper No. 5).

Fougère, D., C. Golfier, G. Horny, E. Kremp. 2012. *Did the 2008 crisis affect the survival of French firms?* Mimeo, Banque de France.

Hall, B.H. 2002. The financing of research and development. *Oxford Review of Economic Policy* 18 (1): 35–51.

Heckman, J. 1979. Sample selection bias as a specification error. *Econometrica* 47 (1): 153–61.

Iyer, R., J.L. Peydró, S. da-Rocha-Lopes, and A. Schoar. 2014. Interbank liquidity crunch and the firm credit crunch: Evidence from the 2007–2009 crisis. *Review of Financial studies* 27 (1): 347–372.

Jaffee, D.M., and T. Russell. 1976. Imperfect information, uncertainty, and credit rationing. *The Quarterly Journal of Economics* 90 (4): 651–666.

Jiménez, G., S. Ongena, J.L. Peydró, and J. Saurina. 2012. Credit supply and monetary policy: Identifying the bank balance-sheet channel with loan applications. *American Economic Review* 102: 2301–2326.

Kirschenmann, K. 2016. Credit rationing in small firm-bank relationships. *Journal of Financial Intermediation* 26: 68–99.

Kremp, E., and P. Sevestre. 2013. Did the crisis induce credit rationing for French SMEs? *Journal of Banking & Finance* 37 (10): 3757–3772.

Leland, H.E., and D.H. Pyle. 1977. Informational asymmetries, financial structure, and financial intermediation. *The Journal of Finance* 32 (2): 371–387.

Levine, R. 2005. Finance and growth: Theory and evidence. In *Handbook of economic growth*, ed. P. Aghion, and S. Durlauf, 865–934. New York: Elsevier North-Holland.

Mancusi, M.L., and A. Vezzulli. 2014. R&D and credit rationing in SMEs. *Economic Inquiry* 52 (3): 1153–1172.

Minetti, R., and S.C. Zhu. 2011. Credit constraints and firm export: Microeconomic evidence from Italy. *Journal of International Economics* 83 (2): 109–125.

Myers, S.C., and N. Majluf. 1984. Corporate financing and investment decisions when firms have information that investors do not have. *Journal of Financial Economics* 13: 187–221.

Ogawa, K., and S.I. Kitasaka. 2000. Bank lending in Japan: Its determinants and macroeconomic implications. In *Crisis and change in the Japanese financial system*, 159–199. US: Springer.

Petersen, M.A., and R.G. Rajan. 1994. The benefits of lending relationships: Evidence from small business data. *The Journal of Finance* 49 (1): 3–37.

Piga, C.A., and G. Atzeni. 2007. R&D investment, credit rationing and sample selection. *Bulletin of Economic Research* 59 (2): 149–178.

Popov, A., and G.F. Udell. 2012. Cross-border banking, credit access, and the financial crisis. *Journal of International Economics* 87 (1): 147–161.

Presbitero, A.F., G.F. Udell, and A. Zazzaro. 2014. The home bias and the credit crunch: A regional perspective. *Journal of Money, Credit and Banking* 46 (s1): 53–85.

Rajan, R.G. 1992. Insiders and outsiders: The choice between informed and arm's-length debt. *The Journal of Finance* 47 (4): 1367–1400.

Scellato, G., and E. Ughetto. 2010. The Basel II reform and the provision of finance for R&D activities in SMEs: An analysis of a sample of Italian companies. *International Small Business Journal* 28 (1): 65–89.

Sette, E., and G. Gobbi. 2015. Relationship lending during a financial crisis. *Journal of the European Economic Association* 13 (3): 453–481.

Shikimi, M. 2005. Do firms benefit from multiple banking relationships? Evidence from small and medium-sized firms in Japan. Institute of Economic Research Hitosubashi University (Working Paper D04–70).

Steijvers, T., and W. Voordeckers. 2009. Collateral and credit rationing: A review of recent empirical studies as a guide for future research. *Journal of Economic Surveys* 23 (5): 924–946.

Stiglitz, J.E., and A. Weiss. 1981. Credit rationing in markets with imperfect information. *The American Economic Review* 71 (3): 393–410.

Thakor, A.V. 1995. Financial intermediation and the market for credit. *Handbooks in Operations Research and Management Science* 9: 1073–1103.

Udell, G.F. 2015. SME access to intermediated credit: What do we know and what don't we know? In Small business conditions and finance: *Proceedings of a conference held in Sydney*, ed. A. Moore on 19–20, 61–109, March 2015, Reserve Bank of Australia, Sydney.

# Authors' Biography

**Paola Brighi** is Associate Professor of Banking and Finance in the Department of Management of the University of Bologna, Italy. She obtained her M.A. from the University of Louvain-la-Neuve and her Ph.D. from the University of Ancona. She has been a visiting scholar at the University of Wisconsin. She is the author of several articles in leading academic journals. She presented her works at many international conferences (Financial Management Association, European Financial Management Association, International Finance and Banking Society, etc.). Her research interests relate to banking structure, relationship lending, bank geographic diversification, efficiency, cooperative banks, and SME finance. She is a member of CEFIN—Center for Studies in Banking and Finance.

**Valeria Venturelli** is Associate Professor in Banking and Finance at the "Marco Biagi" Department of Economics of the University of Modena and Reggio Emilia, where she teaches Financial Markets and Institutions at both undergraduate and graduate level. She graduated in Economics from the University of Modena and Reggio Emilia and received a Ph.D. in Financial Markets and Institutions from the Catholic University of Milan. Her main research interests are the economics of banking and other financial institutions and valuation methods. She is the author of several articles in leading academic journals. She has acted as a consultant to various public institutions and consulting firms. She is a member of CEFIN—Center for Studies in Banking and Finance and Softech-ICT.

# 5

# What Is and What Is not Regulatory Arbitrage? A Review and Syntheses

Magnus Willesson

## 5.1 Introduction

A company may respond to updated regulatory requirements in various ways, which institutional theory defines as regulatory responses and can include a broad spectrum of behaviours from manipulation to compliance (Oliver 1991). However, as noted by VanHoose (2007), this branch of literature does not pay much attention to the occurrence of regulatory arbitrage. Fleischer (2010) suggests that regulatory arbitrage can occur when one of three conditions is met: regulatory-regime inconsistency, economic-substance inconsistency and time inconsistency.[1] Different technical or strategic positions held within or between regulatory policies can generate the same or similar outcomes without considering costs arising from regulatory requirements. Organising

The author wishes to thank Handelsbankens Forskningsstiftelser for providing financial support.

M. Willesson (✉)
Linnæus University, Växjö, Sweden
e-mail: magnus.willesson@lnu.se

**71**
G. Chesini et al. (eds.), *Financial Markets, SME Financing and Emerging Economies*,
Palgrave Macmillan Studies in Banking and Financial Institutions,
DOI 10.1007/978-3-319-54891-3_5

transactions in secured forms (Ambrose et al. 2005), making internal transactions or transferring business activities (including the possibilities on assets or liabilities) to countries with lower regulation standards (Milcheva 2013), are examples of ways in which a company (bank) can exploit the benefits arising from regulatory differences. A company (bank) can act as a regulatory arbitrageur. The most obvious yet very generally described reason to employ regulatory arbitrage is to reduce costs (either financially or operationally relative to risk).

The possible existence of regulatory arbitrage opportunities can be problematic in terms of both financial stability and fairness. Financial stability, including the development of banking activities in non-regulated areas (i.e. the shadow banking system (Milcheva 2013)), can erode control possibilities. Regulatory inconsistency can affect investments due to compliance costs and regulatory risks (Menezes and Roessler 2010) or a reliance on regulatory certifications for determining the return requirements, which can result in underinvestment when regulatory determined risk are overestimated (Berg et al. 2011). The fairness perspective addresses possibilities in which all actors are not treated the same way or do not have the same possibility to utilise the benefits that other actors have. For instance, Knoll (2005) comments on the unfair conditions that result when less wealthy or less sophisticated actors pay higher regulatory costs than wealthier and more sophisticated actors. These factors also influence regulatory arbitrage when an organisation coordinates regulatory supervision globally, as noted by Moshiran (2012).

Although the general attitude towards regulatory arbitrage is negative, some positive outcomes have been identified. Freixas et al. (2007) suggest that regulatory arbitrage may lead to a more efficient use of capital by reducing investment distortions, thus increasing the attractiveness of funds for investments that would otherwise not be allocated due to opportunities to use lower capital cost and as risky assets are transferred to institutions with lower social costs of failure. Another positive view is presented by Berg et al. (2011), who determine that situations in which regulation overestimates risk can adjust deviations by regulatory arbitrage and create a more efficient financial system. It is also shown that regulatory arbitrage opportunities boost interest in adopting new regulatory regimes (e.g. as a consequence of relatively lower capital requirements for selected risks under Basel II than under previous regimes) (cf. Calem and Follain 2007).

Although Carruthers and Lamoreaux (2016) relate regulatory arbitrage to as far back as Adam Smith's theories, the terminology has widely spread as part of the evolution of the Basel II framework for banks. One challenge related to previous regulatory frameworks concerns the fact that the reclassification of assets can reduce capital requirements (Calem and Rob 1999; Kreiner 2002; Lastra 2004). The financial crisis of 2007–2008 has drawn additional attention to regulatory arbitrage after it was found that banks had securitised their assets to avoid the effects of regulatory capital constraints (e.g. Cardone-Riportella et al. 2010).

Despite the increasing attention that regulatory arbitrage has drawn over the past decade, the current knowledge on the existence and use of regulatory arbitrage and on its consequences for stakeholders and society remains limited. Research-wise, regulatory arbitrage is problematic due to a reverse null-hypothesis problem. Regulatory arbitrage is—generally speaking—an action against the effects of regulation. As a result, a statistical test of a hypothesised outcome of regulation does not apply due to non-observed determinations unless an action of regulatory arbitrage addresses a measurable behaviour (e.g. securitisation).

To observe regulatory arbitrage through research, this chapter addresses fundamental discussions on definitions, operationalisations and theories. Solid analyses of regulatory arbitrage hypotheses require both transparent definitions and theoretical relevance. By surveying the existing research on regulatory arbitrage, this chapter discusses the context and scope of regulatory arbitrage to date. This review's focus on regulatory arbitrage research distinguishes it from another recent review on regulatory arbitrage (Carruthers and Lamoreaux 2016) that discussed the concept of regulatory competition. Although this aspect is covered in this review as well, more attention is paid to methodological and theoretical questions, which leads to an institutional focus. The main conclusions drawn from this review are that whereas the literature seems to agree on an implicit understanding of what regulatory arbitrage is, this is less apparent when looking under the surface. The results presented in this chapter suggest that most studies consider regulatory arbitrage to be either something obvious that all should understand (regulatory arbitrage is essentially regulatory arbitrage) or a possible outcome of a scenario (this observation can lead to a scenario of regulatory arbitrage, whatever that is). However, another observation is that regulatory arbitrage is not consistently defined through research when attempts are made. The main discrepancy lies in the assumption that it is a strategic decision or a manoeuvre involving the use of derivatives and financial transactions.

An outline of the literature survey is presented in Sect. 5.2. In separate discussions, this chapter reviews a variety of definitions in Sect. 5.3, theoretical considerations are reviewed in Sect. 5.4 and research approaches are reviewed in Sect. 5.5. Section 5.6 summarises and concludes the findings.

# 5.2    Literature Survey Methodology

This review considers a broad range of research articles that focused on regulatory arbitrage. With its attention to research engagement, this directs the literature search while also limiting its scope. Whereas attention to the contexts in which regulatory arbitrage can occur is not of significant importance, it can be relevant when determining how research must be organised. For instance, the intention is to determine how regulatory arbitrage based on securitisation is analysed in a context of regulatory arbitrage and not to show that securitisation is used to organise regulatory arbitrage in a given regulatory context. The 91-article sample used touches on both institutional and regulatory aspects of regulatory arbitrage problems and a variety of research strategies, concepts, definitions, theories and methodologies used to operationalise such research.

The literature search strategy was carried out based on academic peer-reviewed articles[2] using the Business Source Primer database entering the search term 'regulatory arbitrage'. The search generated in 198 articles (September 2016), but many of these did not appear to serve an academic audience or focused on financial arbitrage and, consequently, not on the institutional management around regulation. The latter also included selection criteria delimitations. Studies discussing questions and perspectives related to regulatory arbitrage were not included unless they discussed regulatory arbitrage explicitly. Consequently, studies on the 'regulatory race to the bottom' or 'securitisation' stemming from literature on regulatory arbitrage did not qualify as a part of the sample unless they addressed regulatory arbitrage explicitly. To limit possible selection or non-selection biases, we complemented the search with (a) alternative search words used to describe regulatory arbitrage in the literature (e.g. structural arbitrage) and (b) searching the reference lists of selected articles. For the latter search, it is worth noting that two articles not explicitly referring to the term 'regulatory arbitrage' were selected. These articles refer to as studying regulatory arbitrage by other studies included in the sample and analyse regulatory arbitrage. Because they do not directly use the terminology regulatory arbitrage, they do not comply with the above-listed selection criteria. However, we are advised by the other author's judgement in the inclusion of these articles. As both of these studies were published late in the study period, we can assume that potential sampling errors resulting from missing important studies are minor. The articles included in the sample were published between 1984 and 2016 (which had not yet ended at the time of the study). To provide an overview of the sample, references are presented graphically with respect to publication years and journal rankings in Fig. 5.1.

It is evident that regulatory arbitrage has been emphasised more intensively since 2004, with sporadic interest occurring prior. The identification of regulatory arbitrage in banking as a result of Basel I and the upcoming regulation in Basel II considering regulatory arbitrage opportunities have been the main drivers of these contributions. This effect extends further as a response to the international financial banking crisis of 2007–2008 that, to a large extent, addressed the uses of securitisation. Peak annual volumes over the sample period occurred in 2013 and 2015 (14 articles). The upcoming regulatory framework included in Basel III has been a recurring focus of articles addressing regulatory arbitrage in contexts of regulatory policies and competition between regulatory systems. This growth in publications will likely continue

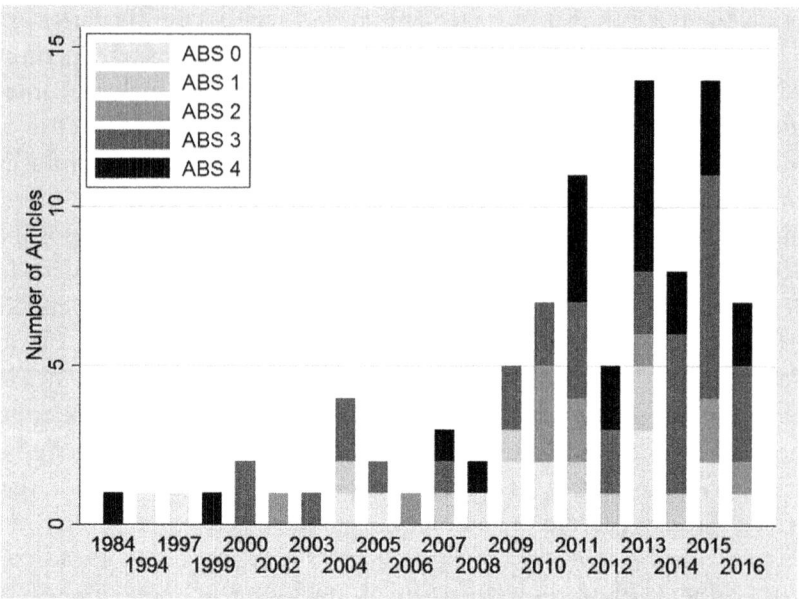

**Fig. 5.1** Number of regulatory arbitrage articles by year and ABS ranking

in banking fields related to the introduction of Basel III, as a result of other regulatory initiatives and will probably spill over to other industries as well.

Studies conducted on the financial sector are overrepresented but not exclusive,[3] consequently affecting the authors' selection of journals. The sampled articles are published in 63 different journals, implying that regulatory arbitrage occurs in various contexts. The journals that are most frequently represented in the sample are the *Journal of Banking and Finance* (13 articles) followed by *The Journal of Financial Economics* (5), *Journal of Real Estate Finance and Economics* and *Journal of Financial Regulation and Compliance* (3). In terms of bibliographic quality classifications, 82%[4] of the references are listed in the 2015 ABS academic journal guide, and most of these are listed under higher-ranking categories. Other than these observations, particular timewise patterns cannot be observed.

**Table 5.1** Summary of sampled article characteristics

|  | Definition | Theory | Hypothesis | Empirical | Securitisation |
|---|---|---|---|---|---|
| Included | 28 | 31 | 22 | 40 | 27 |
| Not included | 63 | 60 | 69 | 51 | 64 |
| Total (N) | 91 | 91 | 91 | 91 | 91 |

Each study was coded based on the following research characteristics: whether the journal defines regulatory arbitrage, cites theories of regulatory arbitrage or at least one regulatory arbitrage hypothesis, or presents an empirical analysis of regulatory arbitrage. A related categorisation involves consideration of securitisation. All of these factors are solely based on an article's attention to regulatory arbitrage. That is, an empirical study only is classified as such if it analyses regulatory arbitrage empirically but not if it includes empirical analyses per se. Summary statistics of these classifications are shown in Table 5.1, and additional analyses of the data introduce each section of this chapter. However, most of the analyses are qualitative and provide both overviews of different perspectives and views on how research on regulatory arbitrage is conducted.

## 5.3 Regulatory Arbitrage: A Survey of Definitions

As stated in the introduction, a general understanding of regulatory arbitrage implies an avoidance strategy based on relative advantages achieved within or between regulatory frameworks. More specific definitions that describe the occurrence of regulatory arbitrage or to analyse operations are rare and inconsistent. In the summary statistics of Table 5.1, 28 studies distinctively define what they mean by regulatory arbitrage, which we review in more detail below. Thirteen of these studies refer to regulatory arbitrage definitions provided by other authors such as Jones (2000) and Houston et al. (2012). Twenty-nine studies do not mention anything related to a definition or even a description of what is meant by the term 'regulatory arbitrage'. The remaining 34 studies can be categorised as describing or using regulatory arbitrage as an outcome or possible outcome of the context addressed (11 studies) or as insinuating the meaning of regulatory arbitrage (23 studies). An example of the latter would be the use of an expression referring to 'exploiting differences between regulatory regimes'. These latter two categories implicitly assume definitions of regulatory arbitrage and seem to assume that readers should know what is meant without being presented with real intentions in the articles. Although this emphasis on regulatory arbitrage definitions does not reflect any timewise patterns, a higher proportion of studies published in higher ranked journals (ABSs 3 and 4) are considering more transparent definitions of regulatory arbitrage.

Definitions expressed in the literature take several directions. Studies emphasising institutional design discuss regulatory arbitrage as part of a regulatory game. Regulatory arbitrage is then defined as a way to avoid regulation. Some observable examples include Boyson et al. (2014b) who frame regulatory arbitrage as 'cherry picking' among assets; Downs and Shi (2015) who define regulatory arbitrage as loopholes in regulations arising from regulatory inconsistency; Aiyar et al. (2014a) who define regulatory arbitrage as a regulatory leakage and Calomiris and Mason (2004) who define the term as a form of safety net abuse and as an opportunity to exploit a gap between market capital requirements and regulatory capital requirements. Another term used is regulatory taxation (Jones 2000), which denotes that an institution's value to its owners is reduced.[5] The purpose of these definitions is to show that regulatory arbitrage is based on opportunities for a company (bank) to avoid regulation. Such arbitrages are found in cross-border activities, whereby banks from countries employing stricter regulations engage with countries employing weaker regulations (Milcheva 2013; Karolyi and Taboada 2015). In addition to suiting managerial needs, this general definition is more likely to be used for interpretations regarding regulatory policies, systemic risks and financial stability levels.

The definitions considered in the literature can, in addition to the above more generalised interpretation of regulatory arbitrage as part of a regulatory game, be based on fundamental differences between regulatory arbitrage as a strategy or strategic choice or be isolated to a transaction taking place. The former view, the *strategy or strategic viewpoint,* addresses managerial positions taken to steer partial or entire operations away from regulations or to avoid the outcomes of regulations imposed in more regulated institutional or geographical areas. This could be applied, for instance, by renaming an operation or business (business line) to suit less regulated conditions or by shifting between different regulatory schemes by utilising firm-specific, country-specific or cross-country differences in regulation (It is not strategic regulatory arbitrage if the organisation under various regulations has other purposes than avoiding effects of regulation). The *transactions viewpoint* relates to financial arbitrage as some form of transaction taking place. The use of derivatives to avoid effects of regulation by reclassifying assets serves as one example.

Let us examine the strategic viewpoint in more detail. Houston et al. (2012) define regulatory arbitrage as the transfer of funds to markets with lower regulations, which are then traded off through institutional quality. In other words, an institution may transfer activities to less regulated markets, but only if satisfying institutional standards are in place. The latter implies that a more heavily regulated market could be preferred over the possibility of capitalising on more lax regulatory requirements. Calem and Follain (2007) discuss regulatory arbitrage as a shift in business strategies (business lines) from one involving more capital requirements to one with lower capital requirements. A definition of regulatory arbitrage that involves adjusting a strategy from high- to low-regulatory environments can also be identified in terms of shadow banking, although this is not limited to the development of a separate shadow-banking system. Kroszner and Strahan (2015) note the possibility of moving businesses 'in the shadow', implying accumulated hidden risks. Accumulation risks lead to aggregated problems later. Acharya et al. (2011) add to this view by defining regulatory arbitrage in terms of a parallel banking system: 'the opportunity for and propensity of the financial sector to adopt organizational forms and financial innovations that would circumvent the regulatory apparatus designed to contain bank risk-taking'. Other studies applying this strategic view are more operationally determined. For instance, Dias (2016) defines regulatory arbitrage as the transfer of risk to a third party to free up capital. Similar definitions are presented by Downs and Shi (2015), who observe that banks find ways to move businesses to subsidiaries controlled by different supervisory regimes in the presence of regulatory arbitrage opportunities and by Aiyar (2014b), who suggests that regulatory arbitrage involves leakage[6] (e.g. shifting lending between subsidiaries that are unequally affected by regulations).

Once regulatory arbitrage opportunities are limited, more control is transferred back to the parent company (bank). Opportunities for regulatory arbitrage may, similar to those of subsidiaries subjected to different regulatory constraints, be defined based on the use of different accounting regulations (Downs and Shi 2015) or based on different measurement characteristics (Galichon 2010; Wang 2016). A difference between standards and reality constitutes another source of regulatory arbitrage (e.g. differences between accounted and real risks) (Blaško and Sinkey 2006; Calomiris and Mason 2004). A definition based on measurement characteristics may focus on regulatory differences (e.g. the various outcomes resulting from standardised and internal ratings methods of the same regulatory (here Basel) framework), estimation of actual risks (e.g. differences in tail risk treatment between Value at Risk methods and Expected Shortfall methods) (Koch-Medina and Munari 2016) or how subadditivity is treated through risk measures (Wang 2016).

Definitions related to transactions focus on particular arrangements (e.g. funds transfers or securities) that avoid regulatory intentions. The literature can be divided into two broad subcategories of this view: one related to transactions taking place and another involving securities. For the first subcategory, incentives for financial innovators to disaggregate and rebundle cash flows to avoid prohibited or disadvantaged transactions serve as one example (Knoll 2005). For the second, Ambrose et al. (2005) suggest that regulatory arbitrage (more precisely regulatory capital arbitrage) is based on a 'decision to hold an asset in securitized form to minimize regulatory capital requirements' and is as such defined based on the technical outcomes of regulatory arbitrage considerations. Partnoy (1997) provides other account of regulatory arbitrage referring to transactions in a securities context: 'regulatory arbitrage consists of those financial transactions designed specifically to reduce costs or capture profit opportunities created by differential regulations or laws'.

Rather than providing strategic and transactional definitions of what regulatory arbitrage is, some studies address regulatory arbitrage in reference to what it is not. Definition-wise, regulatory arbitrage is then determined under the non-arbitrage rule or as opposite to the 'efficient contracting hypothesis' (Calomiris and Mason 2004). Whereas Lysandrou and Nesvetailova (2015) take the 'reaching for yield' position as a contrary standpoint to regulatory arbitrage, Ellul et al. (2014) add to this perspective by defining regulatory arbitrage as either reaching for yields or taking on tail risks in their study of insurance companies. One additional example is based on investor perspective used by Eling and Schemeister (2010) to express a preference for assets that promise higher expected returns as long as they comply with regulatory requirements. By considering these terminologies, such studies imply that companies search for greater risks that are not accounted for in fair value accounting or regulatory bodies.

## 5.4   Review of Theories Associated with Regulatory Arbitrage

Beyond how regulatory arbitrage is defined, research theoretically explains why it exists. We define theory broadly as knowledge on why regulatory arbitrage exists (or why it does not). This distinction is delimited specifically to a theoretical understanding of regulatory arbitrage and does not refer to theories associated with other theories used in other contexts even though the study focuses on regulatory arbitrage applied in another context. Furthermore, we distinguish between theories and hypotheses based on analytical settings. Theories explain behaviours and motives determining why regulatory arbitrage may or may not occur, whereas hypotheses identify sources, determinants or motives for studying the presence of regulatory arbitrage. Theories are consequently required to understand contextual knowledge beyond the existence of determinants of regulatory arbitrage.

In the sample, 31 studies present motivations for contextual knowledge on regulatory arbitrage (vague theoretical discussions or presentations are included in this value). Sixteen of these studies present a clear and direct theoretical explanation, and four studies refer to regulatory arbitrage as a theoretical concept (regulatory arbitrage theory). The remaining 11 studies implicitly explain the theoretical relevance of the analyses conducted. This implies that the remaining 60 articles present nothing on the theoretical value of regulatory arbitrage. Although this is not an indication of theoretical understandings of regulatory arbitrage, a general picture emerges regarding the non-reflective understanding of regulatory arbitrage in analytical terms in line with a prior observation (VanHoose 2007). This picture becomes even clearer when we acknowledge that 22 of the studies present some type of hypothesis on regulatory arbitrage, of which 16 do not present any theories. Consequently, 44 of the studies do not present theories or hypotheses related to regulatory arbitrage.

Cardone-Riportella et al. (2010) present a common reason for theoretical development. The assumption that regulatory arbitrage is utilised whenever such opportunities can be observed: 'If the regulatory capital arbitrage hypothesis holds true, then a financial entity that holds less regulatory capital will have a greater incentive to securitise its assets' (Cardone-Riportella et al. 2010). Consequently, a general approach involves assuming that an identified regulatory arbitrage is also used by all actors capable of using it. Partnoy (1997) suggests that the understanding of arbitrage is the choice of a party to select among a variety of strategies to achieve the same economically equivalent position. In such a context, a regulatory cost to one possible position implies a utilisation of other types of transactions. This can, for instance, be related to regulatory inequalities (by different taxes, accounting requirements, investment restrictions and government subsidies) on non-derivative transactions and its derivative counterparty (e.g. when regulatory restrictions require parties to pay higher prices (including all transactions costs) than for a derivative counterpart).

When it is present in the articles, this form of theoretical irrelevance leads to opportunity cost reasoning, the generation of a regulatory arbitrage hypothesis or simply the conclusion that there are opportunities/risks of regulatory arbitrage. Another way of expressing similar trade-offs involves arguing for the opposite perspective that regulatory arbitrage opportunities will not take place in the event that a theoretical explanation is given. Mingo (2000) describes the existence of theories based on regulatory principles as follows:

> so long as the "approved" internal models were precisely the same ones being used by banks for their daily business decisions (a good idea, in any event, to forestall "gaming" of the FM approach), the incentive to engage in regulatory capital arbitrage would disappear.[7] (Mingo 2000)

The view that regulatory arbitrage is used when it is present is not only considered an assumption in the literature. Regulatory arbitrage is argued to be a theoretical concept or rather as the presence of a theory of non-arbitrage (Wang 2016). Although not discussed explicitly, such a theory is based on a number of assumptions related to stakeholder decisions made when alternatives are given and self-interest decisions made at the expense of other stakeholders.

As noted by VanHoose (2007), the regulatory implications of bank behaviour under regulation diverge. Regulatory arbitrage only constitutes part of this explanation. There are additional factors to consider and understanding these factors requires maintaining a balancing act between different opportunity costs.

A possible neoclassical approach to regulatory arbitrage addresses company (bank) decisions by matching risks through an overall optimal balance sheet strategy that involves assets and capitalisation.[8] Riskiness is driven by the franchise value of a bank. Consequently, when capital driven by stakeholders' preferences generates higher value, the bank will have more to lose in the event of, for instance, the development of valuable relationships or a profitable deposit base. The basic assumption of regulatory arbitrage use is to come closer to the strategic optimal risk level when it is affected by regulatory constraints.[9] From the sampled literature, we observe explanations of regulatory arbitrage as the securitisation of assets not subject to the same regulatory constraints of a securitised form (Ambrose et al. 2005), as strategic adjustments made between asset categories in an asset portfolio depending on their importance for risk measures relative to actual risks (Berg et al. 2011) or as the presence of subadditivity in measurement approaches. However, these aspects may result in positive outcomes when risks are divided into different operative units/affiliates (Wang 2016).

Another theoretical approach involves discussing regulatory arbitrage as regulatory development or as a 'regulatory game'. For instance, Barkin (2015) discusses regulatory arbitrage based on regulatory heterogeneity. The analytical foundation presented is based on regulatory competition between nations that leads to a 'regulatory race to the bottom' where free capital will move to the country (or area) imposing the lowest regulatory barriers. In this set-up, financial institutions are considered 'regulatory buyers' and 'buy' the country with the lowest regulations. Consequently, nations limit regulations to attract capital, and this ultimately results in a global downward harmonisation of regulations. However, the reduction of regulatory requirements (and associated cost advantages) and search for the lowest levels of regulation are weighted against positive outcomes of regulation. For instance, nations limit regulations to attract capital but are balanced by an upward adjustment in regulation based on market power from richer countries, international harmonisation (the headquarters' regulatory compliance with the home market is spread out across other countries) and normative discursive preferences. Under such conditions, reputations, quality of services to economic actors and access to key markets counterbalance regulatory competition. To a company, this serves as similar reasoning as efficient contracting, which presents barriers based on agency costs (Harvard Law Review 2004). Efficient contracting theory can explain or rather explain the opposite of the use of regulatory arbitrage (Cardone-Riportella et al. 2010) (e.g. the level of deposit insurance relative to the cost of financial distress or when banks bearing the costs of financial distress use securitisation less, thus presenting an opposite hypothesis from that of regulatory arbitrage). The reviewed literature identifies (implicitly or explicitly) a number of determinants of regulatory arbitrage related to contracting theories (e.g. efficient contracting (Calomiris and Mason 2004), a race for yields (Lysandrou and Nesvetailova 2015), reputations (Ambrose et al. 2005) and regulatory reach (Jain et al. 2013)). Agency costs and strategic behaviours add transaction costs to the regulatory decisions discussed above. This can be expressed in terms of institutional fostering (through financial innovation, corporate conglomeration and the rise of the regulatory state) or of a lack of transparency (Harvard Law Review 2004). Similar expressions are identified through trade theory in reference to comparative advantages (Fung et al. 2011) and spillover effects (Carbo-Valverde et al. 2012; Ongena et al. 2013). By extension, Fleischer (2010) discusses the costs of arbitrage from a legal perspective in a discussion on balancing transaction costs with regulatory costs. Considerations of regulatory arbitrage (and tax avoidance) may distort a company's decision-making and regulatory acceptance. Opportunities to minimise transaction costs may result in regulatory costs in the short or long term, and the use of regulatory arbitrage is dependent on whether regulatory development occurs to reduce regulatory or transactions costs (Fleischer 2010: 275). Explanations result in empirical observations depending on ownership characteristics.

## 5.5   Review of Empirical Research Designs (Empirical Data and Methods)

Empirical research of any form was conducted in less than half (44%) of the sampled studies. These studies are of course significantly associated (based on a chi-square test) with the presentation of a regulatory arbitrage hypothesis. However, the generation or discussion of regulatory arbitrage hypotheses does not necessarily involve conducting empirical studies or tests. Hypotheses are also the focus of descriptive analyses or theoretical models without empirical considerations. Securitisation is the focus of 12 empirical studies, and as shown in Sect. 5.3, the approach can be used to define regulatory arbitrage. However, not all studies focusing on securitisation actually address regulatory arbitrage based on securitisation settings. From an empirical standpoint, this further denotes that more than twice as many studies (28 to be exact) do not consider aspects of securitisation at all. The 40 empirical studies based on empirical data include data series for 1973–2012, and most of the studies are based on data on US or European countries or a combination thereof and are to a large extent published in journals ranked 3 (16) or 4 (14).

Empirical research is diverse and methodological approaches to empirical research vary. A few of the empirical studies aim at furthering knowledge on regulatory arbitrage and approach this through sensitivity analyses (López-Andión et al. 2015), interviews (MacKenzie 2011; Liu 2015) and questionnaires (Dhanani et al. 2007). Most of the empirical studies aim to present a determinant/association (including tests of hypotheses) between regulatory arbitrage and of other variables. Determinations of the occurrence of regulatory arbitrage can be identified through case illustrations (Blundall-Wignal and Atkinson 2009) or from data approximations. Some examples of the latter are presented by Agostino and Mazzuca (2011), who aim at deriving the use of regulatory arbitrage based on the level of securitisation that is in turn approximated by Tier 1 capital and by Milcheva (2013), who examines variations in balance sheets to determine the supply of securitised credit in the economy. One straightforward approach consequently involves using a variable to approximate regulatory arbitrage. Such cases involve the use of securitisation while assuming that the use (or increased use) of a specific security or type of transaction serves as an indication of regulatory arbitrage. Key ratios are alternative approximations of behaviour that can be used to measure regulatory arbitrage. Acharya and Steffen (2015) analyse a positive effect in the ratio between risk-weighted assets (RWA) and assets to determine regulatory arbitrage as an investment motive of risky sovereign debt.

As observed in prior sections of this chapter, empirical observations of strategic regulatory arbitrage are not necessarily as straightforward as transactions related to regulatory arbitrage. In contrast to analysing regulatory arbitrage variables based on a variable proxy, determinations and implications are analysed indirectly based on rough estimates or assumptions. As noted in the introduction, regulatory arbitrage can (but not necessarily) constitute a non-action of a suggested change. Consequently, an absence of outcomes can be used to test hypotheses related to regulatory arbitrage. For instance, Acharya et al. (2013) consider the absence of a relation between the regulatory capital ratio and conduit activity and Cardone-Riportella et al. (2010) interpret the opposite of the efficient contracting hypothesis as the outcome of regulatory arbitrage. A few studies emphasise the effects of economic factors. Aiyar et al. (2014a, b), in examining the lending sector, compare studied banks to a reference group and Ambrose et al. (2005) test a variety of hypotheses related to regulatory behaviours based on the performance of securitised and non-securitised loans. The latter approach is used to verify the results as determined by information asymmetries or actually a regulatory arbitrage. This raises the possibility of drawing conclusions regarding the existence of strategic regulatory arbitrage to exclude the possibility of all other explanations for non-action. As one example from the literature, Ongena et al. (2013) use a number of control variables to validate the occurrence of regulatory spillover effects.

## 5.6   Conclusions

By surveying and reviewing 91 research articles on regulatory arbitrage, this chapter identifies how the literature defines, theorises on and studies regulatory arbitrage empirically. Most articles consider banking and financial markets for several reasons: the international organisation of capital flows in both real and securitised forms, the intensified regulatory control of capital flows and of their institutions and the identification of regulatory arbitrage opportunities as part of the analytical field emerging after the financial crisis of 2007–2008. It can be concluded that many studies consider regulatory arbitrage as a matter of course both in terms of how regulatory arbitrage is defined and in terms of how it is treated theoretically.

We thus first conclude from our literature review that regulatory arbitrage is not consistently defined in research articles. Based on our literature survey, we can classify regulatory arbitrage as either related to strategies or as directed towards technical conditions of financial derivatives/securitisation. However, the use of broad, vague and sweeping definitions of regulatory arbitrage limits opportunities to conduct theoretical and empirical research and limits the opportunities of causally determining when regulatory arbitrage does or does not apply. This includes determinations of what regulatory arbitrage is not.

Although most studies seem to apply an implicit understanding of regulatory arbitrage, this becomes less apparent when looking beyond the surface appearances.

Theoretically speaking, from this review we can conclude that both institutional and policy-related theories apply to regulatory arbitrage. Several studies exploit opportunities to balance decisions regarding whether regulatory institutions or companies/banks use regulatory arbitrage. Applying both neoclassical theory and agency-theoretical perspectives reveals opportunity costs that both regulators and institutions assume in regards to regulation and considers factors of relevance for both transactions costs and institutional costs and benefits. Part of the literature considers regulatory arbitrage itself as a theoretical construct but does not explain the motives behind regulatory arbitrage strategy adoption.

Empirically speaking, research challenges concern assumptions and definitions. Strategic actions benefitting from regulatory loopholes are difficult to measure but serve as possible outcomes of hypothesis tests. This limitation is attributable to the fact that regulatory arbitrage constitutes a form of avoidance (non-action). At the same time, we can conclude that empirical analyses are more straightforward when it is possible to study a change in a measure related to regulatory arbitrage such as defined measurements of a securitised position or key ratio. This implies that transaction-based forms of regulatory arbitrage are more operational when conducting research than strategic forms of regulatory arbitrage. Although empirically oriented methodologies are only briefly reviewed in this chapter, further methodological development is welcome. For instance, in terms of measuring causal effects, these definitions have a 'non-action' relation to exogenous factors.

Research on regulatory arbitrage is currently in its infancy. The findings and conclusions drawn from this review observe operative definitions related to certain types of transactions but at the same time highlight opportunities to develop knowledge on regulatory arbitrage. It is likely that regulatory arbitrage will persist in the future regardless of which regulatory framework is in place, and additional studies must be conducted to learn more on this issue. Existing and additional theoretical knowledge on regulatory arbitrage can further regulatory development while introducing new views on institutional development. While a number of research challenges have been addressed, some remain to be addressed in the future. More precise definitions could further both empirical research and eclectic theoretical understanding, thus adding value to analyses of this issue for company and regulatory development. This will also further analyses of securitisation scenarios and of strategies that are not necessarily designed to arbitrage on regulatory shortfalls.

## Notes

1. Regulatory-regime inconsistency implies that the same transactions receive different regulatory treatment under different regulatory regimes. Economic-substance inconsistency implies that two transactions with the same cash flow receive different treatment under the same regulatory regime. Time inconsistency denotes that the same transaction receives different regulatory treatment at different points in time (i.e. the future).

2. As only academic literature is addressed, we exclude documentation and discussions of regulatory arbitrage by regulatory authorities (e.g. BIS/EBA). Academically oriented book chapters (e.g. Willesson 2016) and working papers (e.g. Boyson et al. 2014a) known to the author are not included in the quantitative analysis. However, these studies and reports serve as helpful contributions for analysing theories and definitions.

3. For instance, Miller et al. (2013) discuss regulatory arbitrage in terms of health insurance, but draw comparisons between regulatory arbitrage and that of the financial sector, and Siegel et al. (2013) discuss regulatory arbitrage in an environment protection setting.

4. ABS refers to the academic journal guide developed by the Association of Business Schools, UK. Note that some of the non-ranked journals are related to academic fields other than business studies.

5. Please observe that Mehran and Thakor (2011) propose that the bank owners' value does not decrease as the cost of equity decreases to compensate for a higher reliance on equity funding due to regulation. Consequently, an owner faces a lower level of risk and should expect an equivalent lower return on the equity invested.

6. According to Aiyar (2014b), who studies loans, regulatory arbitrage is one out of three forms of leakage along with effects of the competition

(foreign branches take over businesses from affected banks) and capital markets channels (entering capital markets as a substitute for bank loans).
7. The FM approach is short for the Full Models approach and refers to the use of bank internal measurement models for risk measurements as approved by supervisors.
8. A thorough description of a neoclassical approach is provided in the working paper (hence not included in the sample) by Boyson et al. (2014a), assuming no agency costs.
9. Willesson (2016) adds to this assumption by suggesting that regulatory arbitrage may be used by banks operating at an optimal level. Restrictive regulatory capital requirements may influence the optimal cushion or signalling of bank solvency to stakeholders even if it does not have direct effects on the capital level.

# References

Acharya, V.V., T. Cooley, M. Richardson, R. Sylla, and I. Walter. 2011. The Dodd-Frank wall street reform and consumer protection act: Accomplishments and limitations. *Journal of Applied Corporate Finance* 23 (1): 43–56.

Acharya, V.V., P. Schnabl, and G. Suarez. 2013. Securitization without risk transfer. *Journal of Financial Economics* 107 (3): 515–536.

Acharya, V.V., and S. Steffen. 2015. The "greatest" carry trade ever? Understanding eurozone bank risks. *Journal of Financial Economics* 115 (2): 2015–2236.

Agostino, M., and M. Mazzuca. 2011. Empirical investigation of securitisation drivers: The case of Italian banks. *The European Journal of Finance* 17 (8): 623–648.

Aiyar, S., C.W. Calomiris, and T. Wieladek. 2014a. Does Macro-Prudential regulation leak? Evidence from a UK policy experiment. *Journal of Money Credit and Banking,* 46 (1, Suppl.): 181–186.

Aiyar, S., C.W. Calomiris, and T. Wieladek. 2014b. Identifying channels of credit substitution when bank capital requirements are varied. *Economic Policy* 29 (77): 45–77.

Ambrose, B.W., M. Lacour-Little, and A.B. Sanders. 2005. Does capital arbitrage, reputation, or asymmetric information drive Securitisation? *Journal of Financial Services Research* 28(1/2/3): 113–133.

Barkin, J.S. 2015. Racing all over the place: A dispersion model of international regulatory competition. *European Journal of International Relations* 21 (1): 171–193.

Berg, T., B. Gehra, and M. Kunisch. 2011. A certification model for regulatory arbitrage: Will regulatory arbitrage persist under Basel III? *The Journal of Fixed Income* 21 (2): 39–56.

Blaško, M., and Sinkey J.F., Jr. 2006. Bank asset structure, real-estate lending, and risk-taking. *The Quarterly Review of Economics and Finance* 46 (1): 53–81.

Blundall-Wignal, A., and P. Atkinson. 2009. Origins of the financial crisis and requirements for reform. *Journal of Asian Economics* 20 (5): 536–548.

Boyson, N.M., R. Fahlenbrach, and R.M. Stulz. 2014a. Why do banks practice regulatory arbitrage? Evidence from usage of trust preferred securities, *Working paper, National Bureau of Economic Research*. http://www.nber.org/papers/w19984. Accessed 30 Sep 2015.

Boyson, N., J. Helwege, and J. Jindra. 2014b. Crises, liquidity shocks, and fire sales at commercial banks. *Financial Management* 43 (4): 857–884.

Calem, P.J., and J.R. Follain. 2007. Regulatory capital arbitrage and the potential competitive impact of Basel II in the market for residential mortgages. *Journal of Real Estate Finance & Economics* 35 (2): 197–219.

Calem, P.J., and R. Rob. 1999. The impact of capital-based regulation on bank risk-taking. *Journal of Financial Intermediation* 8 (4): 317–352.

Calomiris, C.W., and J.R. Mason. 2004. Credit card securitization and regulatory arbitrage. *Journal of Financial Services Research* 26 (1): 5–27.

Carbo-Valverde, S., E.J. Kane, and F. Rodriguez-Fernandez. 2012. Regulatory arbitrage in cross-border banking mergers within the EU. *Journal of Money, Credit and Banking* 44 (8): 1609–1629.

Cardone-Riportella, C., R. Samaniego-Medina, and A. Trujillo-Ponce. 2010. What drives bank securitisation? The Spanish experience. *Journal of Banking and Finance* 34 (11): 2639–2651.

Carruthers, B.G., and N.R. Lamoreaux. 2016. Regulatory races: The effects of jurisdictional competition on regulatory standards. *Journal of Economic Literature* 54 (1): 52–97.

Dhanani, A., S. Fifield, C. Helliar, and L. Stevenson. 2007. Why UK companies hedge interest rate risk. *Studies in Economics and Finance* 24 (1): 72–90.

Dias, R. 2016. Credit default Swaps: Has the GFC influenced perceptions of their utility for banks. *Journal of Economic Surveys* 30 (4): 712–735.

Downs, D.H., and L. Shi. 2015. The impact of reversing regulatory arbitrage on loan originations: Evidence from bank holding companies. *Journal of Real Estate Finance and Economics* 50 (3): 307–338.

Eling, M., and H. Schemeister. 2010. Insurance and the credit crisis: Impact and ten consequences for risk management and supervision. *The Geneva Papers* 35 (1): 9–34.

Ellul, A., C. Jotikasthira, and C.T. Lundblad. 2014. Mark-to-market accounting and systemic risk: Evidence from the insurance industry. *Economic Policy* 29 (78): 297–341.

Fleischer, V. 2010. Regulatory arbitrage. *Texas Law Review* 89 (2): 228–290.

Freixas, X., G. Lóránth, and A.D. Morrison. 2007. Regulating financial conglomerates. *Journal of Financial Intermediation* 16 (4): 479–514.

Fung, H.-G., J. Yau, and G. Zhang. 2011. Reported trade figure discrepancy, regulatory arbitrage, and round-tripping: Evidence from the China-Hong Kong trade data. *Journal of International Business Studies* 42 (1): 152–176.

Galichon, A. 2010. The VAR at risk. *International Journal of Theoretical and Applied Finance* 13 (4): 503–505.

Harvard Law Review. (2004). Investor liability financial innovations in the regulatory state and the coming revolution in corporate law 117 (8): 1841–1958.

Houston, J.F., C. Lin, and Y. Ma. 2012. Regulatory arbitrage and international bank flows. *The Journal of Finance* 67 (5): 1845–1895.

Jain, A., P. Jain, T.H. McInish, and M. McKenzie. 2013. Worldwide reach of short selling regulations. *Journal of Financial Economics* 109 (1): 177–197.

Jones, D. 2000. Emerging problems with the Basel Capital Accord: Regulatory capital arbitrage and related issues. *Journal of Banking & Finance* 24 (1/2): 35–58.

Karolyi, G.A., and A.G. Taboada. 2015. Regulatory arbitrage and cross-border bank acquisitions. *The Journal of Finance* 70 (6): 2395–2450.

Knoll, M.S. 2005. Regulatory arbitrage using put-call parity. *Journal of Applied Finance* 15 (1): 64–74.

Koch-Medina, P., and C. Munari. 2016. Unexpected shortfalls of expected shortfall: Extreme default profiles and regulatory arbitrage. *Journal of Banking & Finance* 62: 141–151.

Kreiner, R.E. 2002. Banking in a theory of the business cycle: A model and critique of the Basle Accord on risk-based capital requirements for banks. *International Review of Law and Economics* 21 (4): 413–433.

Kroszner, R.S., and P.E. Strahan. 2015. Financial regulatory reform: Challenges ahead. *American Economic Review: Papers & Proceedings* 101 (3): 242–246.

Lastra, R.M. 2004. Risk-based capital requirements and their impact upon the banking industry: Basel II and Cad III. *Journal of Financial Regulation and Compliance* 12 (3): 225–239.

Liu, X. 2015. How institutional and organizational characteristics explain the growth of contingent work in China. *ILR Review* 68 (2): 372–387.

López-Andión, C., A. Iglesias-Casal, M.C. López-Penabad, and J.M. Maside-Sanfiz. 2015. The solvency of financial institutions in Spain: Lessons from securitization. *Applied Economics* 47 (44): 4741–4753.

Lysandrou, P., and A. Nesvetailova. 2015. The role of shadow banking entities in the financial crisis: A disaggregated view. *Review of International Political Economy* 22 (2): 257–279.

MacKenzie, D. 2011. The credit crisis as a problem in the sociology of knowledge. *American Journal of Sociology* 116 (6): 1778–1841.

Mehran, H., and A. Thakor. 2011. Bank capital and value in the cross-section. *The Review of Financial Studies* 24 (4): 1019–1067.

Menezes, F.M., and C. Roessler. 2010. Good and bad consistency in regulatory decisions. *The Economic Record* 86 (275): 504–516.

Milcheva, S. 2013. Cross-country effects of regulatory capital arbitrage. *Journal of Banking & Finance* 37 (12): 5329–5345.

Miller, A.R., C. Eibner, and C.R. Gresenz. 2013. Financing of employer sponsored health insurance plans before and after health reform: What consumers don't know won't hurt them? *International Review of Law and Economics* 36: 36–47.

Mingo, J.J. 2000. Policy implications of the federal reserve study of credit risk models at major US banking institutions. *Journal of Banking & Finance* 24 (1): 15–33.

Moshiran, F. 2012. The future and dynamics of global systemically important banks. *Journal of Banking & Finance* 36 (10): 2675–2679.

Oliver, C. 1991. Strategic responses to institutional processes. *Academy of Management Review* 16 (1): 145–179.

Ongena, S., A. Popov, and G.F. Udell. 2013. "When the cat's away the mice will play": Does regulation at home affect bank risk-taking abroad? *Journal of Financial Economics* 108 (3): 727–750.

Partnoy, F. 1997. Financial derivatives and the cost of regulatory arbitrage. *The Journal of Corporation Law* 22 (2): 212–256.

Siegel, J.I., A.N. Licht, and S.H. Schwartz. 2013. Egalitarianism, cultural distance and foreign direct investment: A new approach. *Organization Science* 24 (4): 1174–1194.

VanHoose, D. 2007. Market discipline and supervisory discretion in banking: Reinforcing or conflicting pillars of Basel II? *Journal of Applied Finance* 17 (2): 105–118.

Wang, R. 2016. Regulatory arbitrage of risk measures. *Quantitative Finance* 16 (3): 337–347.

Willesson, M. 2016. A note on regulatory arbitrage: Bank risk, capital risk, interest rate risk and ALM in European banking. In *Liquidity risk, efficiency and new bank business models,* ed. S. Carbó Valverde, P.J. Cuadros Solas, and F. Rodríguez Fernandez. Houndmills: Palgrave Macmillan. ISBN: 978-3-319-30819-7.

# Author Biography

**Magnus Willesson** is Senior Lecturer at Linnæus University, Växjö, Sweden, and visiting fellow at University of Essex, Colchester, UK. He obtained his Ph.D. from the University of Gothenburg, Sweden. The teaching experience includes banking, financial institutions and markets, strategic risk management and corporate finance. The research emphasises how risk, efficiency and governance of actors in the financial sector are affected by changing environments (such as technology, market changes, regulations or management requirements). It is published in several international journals and as book chapters covering subjects such as risk-taking and risk management in banks, banking efficiency, operational risk in banks, the banks' adoption of the Basel II and Basel III accords and the cost-efficiency and pricing of payments.

# 6

# Forecasting Models and *Probabilistic Sensitivity Analysis*: An Application to Bank's Risk Appetite Thresholds Within the *Risk Appetite Framework*

Maurizio Polato, Josanco Floreani,
Giuseppe Giannelli and Nicola Novielli

## 6.1    Introduction

Following the great financial crisis a great effort was taken by supervisors around the world in order to foster and strengthen banks' corporate governance mechanisms. Regulatory breaches and sharp declines in banks' standards of conduct were the main concerns prompting widespread and far-reaching regulatory responses.

As known, banks were first required to strengthen their capital adequacy levels under the Basel Capital accords with the primary goal of reinforcing protections against unexpected losses. In the meanwhile, efforts were made in order to cope with risk management issues. Actually, one of the key points that the crisis underpinned was a lack of adequate risk reporting standards (Grody and Hughes 2016).

M. Polato (✉) · J. Floreani · G. Giannelli · N. Novielli
University of Udine, Udine, Italy
e-mail: maurizio.polato@uniud.it

© The Author(s) 2017                                                                     **95**
G. Chesini et al. (eds.), *Financial Markets, SME Financing and Emerging Economies*,
Palgrave Macmillan Studies in Banking and Financial Institutions,
DOI 10.1007/978-3-319-54891-3_6

The Financial Stability Board (FSB) was heavily involved in providing guidelines and recommendations for improving on risk management issues for banking institutions. The FSB reports set down the basic principles of the so-called Risk Appetite Framework-RAF (FSB 2013a, b). The RAF captured an increasing interest of supervisors (see CRMPG 2008; BCBS 2009; SSG 2010; CEBS 2010; FSB 2013a, b; Central Bank of Ireland 2014), practitioners and, to a lesser extent, academic scholars. One of the most challenging regulatory mandates, however, is that under BCBS 239 requiring banks to implement robust arrangements on risk data aggregation and reporting.

The RAF emerges as an important tool for risk management and control in a rapidly changing environment where strategic planning processes in banking institutions even more requires the support of models, which allow measuring the impact of different scenarios.

A rapidly changing environment coupled with an evolving regulatory framework urges banks to rely on simulation-based forecasting model in order to assess bank soundness and capital adequacy under stressed scenarios. Actually, introducing advanced statistical techniques in decision-making processes becomes particularly compelling for managing uncertainty surrounding both exogenous and bank's policy variables.

Under this perspective, therefore, the system of risks in banking institutions is no more a mere by-product of financial planning; rather it becomes a fundamental part of strategic planning permeating all management and risk control processes, involving all the functions. In that, the RAF is a step behind traditional forecasting models. In fact, while the latter just summarize strategy in quantitative variables, the RAF emerges as a managerial and monitoring tool linking risk objectives to the overall bank's operations and strategies.

The aim of this chapter is to discuss the rationale of a Risk Appetite Framework as implemented by the Bank of Italy with its Circular 263/2006 as subsequently amended and updated. More precisely, we present the methodological basics of the framework and their strategic and policy implications for bank's risk management. Within this perspective, the work is intended to investigate the possible applications of a probabilistic forecasting model within a Risk Appetite Framework.

The work is organized as follows. Section 6.2 presents the rationale of the framework. Section 6.3 discusses a possible methodological approach to probabilistic analysis. Section 6.4 proposes an example with reference to the TCR and ROE as output parameters. Section 6.5 concludes.

## 6.2   The Rationale of a Risk Appetite Framework

The financial crisis leads regulators and supervisors to redefine the basic principles of risk management and risk control with the aim of preserving bank's soundness and reducing the risks of systemic adverse effects of bank crisis. This involves a renewed interest on sound corporate governance practices and internal controls. Basically, banks are required to adopt a formalized framework guiding risk management and monitoring practices.

By the way, it is widely recognized the link between risk-taking (or excessive risk-taking), default risk, distress costs and bank value. The link between risk management, bank strategy and governance is straightforward as well. Distress costs arise as financial distress makes the bank no longer able to pursue its strategy. Under the shareholder value-maximization perspective, therefore, the risk of financial distress is the risk to be managed.

The shareholder maximization argument has been raised by Stulz (2016) who developed a framework where there is for each bank a level of risk leading to bank's value maximization. An effective corporate governance takes the responsibility to assure that the management chooses the level of risk which maximizes shareholder wealth under regulatory constraints, with the latter defining the bank's risk capacity.[1]

The aforementioned links and relations among the various levels of risk management and governance precisely help shaping the concept of the Risk Appetite Framework.

Put it in general terms, the RAF approach designs a multifaceted framework comprising "polices, processes, controls and systems through which the risk appetite is established, communicated and monitored" (FSB 2013a). The rationale of the framework is to limit bank's risk-taking to its capacity of absorbing and managing risks.

Despite not stating any clear relation or hierarchy between the above-mentioned concepts (Baldan et al. 2014), the approach to risk management envisaged by the FSB reports elicit a few considerations. It leads to an affirmation of far-reaching corporate governance culture. More precisely, it supports the strategic decision-making process and capital allocation. In that, it helps aligning operations in view of achieving bank's strategic goals. It, then, serves the purpose of setting a framework of operational limits to credit risk, market risk and other risks. Next, it helps guiding a coherent transposition of strategic goals across different business units within budgetary and decision-making processes. Finally, but not less important, the RAF is a perquisite for communication purposes to the stakeholders.

The key point of aligning RAF with strategic goals is allowing banks to embed both risk and return considerations into strategic decision-making. Relating strategic goals and the correlated return targets within the bank's actual and desired risk profile stands at the heart of a sound ERM where different risk management features are integrated in a holistic manner (Alix et al. 2015).

Actually, implementing an effective ERM system has far-reaching implications spanning risk management and accounting policies. It has been argued (Grody and Hughes 2016) that the proper implementation of BCBS 239 compellingly requires the adoption of a common risk metric for all types of risk. Such a goal involves both risk managers and accountants, envisaging a two pillar approach which claims forcing to the convergence of finance and risk systems within a unique control and reporting system and the implementation of a common risk measurement framework. Such an approach points to the integration of both risk and accounting data into a single framework which can be referred as to "Risk Accounting". Several implications of a Risk Accounting framework have been recognized, ranging from the determination of regulatory capital requirements, the calculation of risk-adjusted performance measure such as RAROC to adjusting betas in the CAPM (Fernandes et al. 2013).

Ultimately, the framework puts risks at the heart of the banks growth strategies and claims for a coherent definition of bank's risk appetite.

Central in bank's risk management under an RAF environment are the concepts of risk tolerance and risk appetite, although banking institutions and supervisors do not unanimously define them. Put it simply, risk tolerance can be regarded as the amount of risk that the bank is willing to accept. Alternatively, a distinction is often made between the "absolute risk which a bank a priory is open to take (Risk appetite) and the actual limits (Risk Tolerance) within the Risk Appetite which the bank pursues" (Basel Committee on Banking Supervision 2009). Such a distinction is envisaged by the FSB itself, although it does not provide a definition of risk tolerance.

Risk Tolerance can be defined as the maximum allowed deviance from the risk appetite (Bank of Italy, Circular 263/2006). Such a threshold is set in view of allowing banks continuing operations within their risk capacity, even under stressed scenarios. Risk capacity, in turn, is defined as the maximum risk a bank can assume without breaching regulatory constraints or other constraints eventually imposed by shareholders or supervisors.

Being designed in accordance with bank's risk capacity, the RAF should be, therefore, coherent with bank's business model, its strategic plan and integrated within the Internal Capital Adequacy Assessment Process (ICAAP).

At a corporate level, the rationale of the RAF lays in identifying both risk objectives (Risk Appetite) and the maximum acceptable deviance (Risk Tolerance) for all major risk categories (credit risk, financial risk, operational risk, reputation risk and other risks such as strategic and legal risk) and Key Performance Indicators (capital adequacy, earnings volatility, shareholder value, risk-adjusted performance metrics, creditworthiness, regulatory standing). Finally, corporate-level risk appetite and tolerances are drilled down to departments and products, each carrying its risk limits and targets.

Widening the perspective, risk analysis leads banks to define a set of operational limits together with identifying clear monitoring responsibilities within their internal control processes in accordance with bank's policies. Defining, risk appetite, risk tolerance and risk limits becomes an important challenge.

Actually, the main contributions come from practitioners with a few works describing the overall architecture of risk governance and management (Booz&Co 2009; IIF 2011; KPMG 2013; GARP 2013) while others focusing on the rationale of risk limits and buffers or proposing specifications on model's parameters (Protiviti 2012; RIMS 2012).

A body of literature, then, takes a more quantitative approach envisaging ways for operationalizing the quantitative features of an RAF model (Cortez 2011; Cremonino 2011; The Society of Actuaries in Ireland 2011; Baldan et al. 2016).

On a methodological ground, two main approaches to RAF are emerging. The first is coherent with the ICAAP framework and defines the risk appetite and the risk tolerance in terms of incidence of total internal capital on total capital. The second approach focuses on the *four legs* methodology. Basically, it consists in defining an upper and a lower risk appetite limit, each coupled with the related trigger. The area between the upper and lower triggers represents the desired range for the risk profile, while a breaching of any of the triggers implies that risk profile is approaching the risk appetite limits requiring corrective actions (see IRM 2011; ECR—EMEA 2013).

By the way, defining a set of operational limits might lead to the implementation of an early warning system prompting bank's management to adopt proper actions and measures in view of reverting to the desired risk-taking levels whenever the bank is approaching any risk limit (McNish et al. 2013).

While regulators miss to set down a methodological framework for thresholds calculation (and, in particular, the risk tolerance), they state as a guideline that the overall RAF architecture should fit the bank's size and its complexity in terms of business model and operations.

Broadly speaking, the approach to risk appetite and risk limits might develop under a determinist environment or, alternatively, under a stochastic and simulation-based approach.

Actually, the implementation of a probabilistic approach to bank's strategic planning under a RAF brings significant improvements to a pure deterministic environment. A deterministic approach, for example, does not allow to perform stress test-based sensitivity analysis unless generating conflicts when defining and interpreting adverse scenarios. For example, while directly sustaining profitability loan portfolio growth increases risk and therefore negatively affects profitability itself. Whether the growth in the loan portfolio is desirable or not is a tricky question which should be solved by firstly defining the target measure to address.

Under a stochastic perspective, by contrast, the RAF becomes a powerful approach to the extent that it integrates forecasting model and sensitivity probabilistic analysis into a model which brings together the strategic dimension, sensitivity analysis and risk measurement and control.

Different approaches and models for strategic planning purposes can be envisaged. Among them, of particular interest are the so-called enterprise-based forecasting models, which allow for investigating the impact of strategies on bank's performance under changing scenarios. Basically, these models simulate balance sheet, profit and loss account, risk exposure and capital absorption given regulatory or managerial constraints. In that, a simulation based forecasting model mapping the wide net of relations among risk parameters can return the risk profile which is implied in bank's strategic choices.

The Bank of Italy precisely supports such a perspective requiring performing stress test analysis in order to assess the effect of adverse scenarios, each characterized by a certain probability, on bank's soundness and profitability.

Moreover, a stochastic approach is particularly suitable to manage and control risks under a Risk Appetite Framework where risk is defined in terms of a system of output measures whose precise specification is essential in order to manage conflicts when defining and interpreting adverse scenarios. A stochastic framework, in fact, allows managing multidimensional models.

Methodologically, a probabilistic approach to sensitivity analysis requires defining the joint distribution of the input variables and, therefore, the outputs. However, defining a joint probability distribution of variables is not always an easy task. An alternative model is to assume univariate probability distributions (and mutually independent) for each variable and, then, employ a copula method according to one of its various specifications (see, among others, Rubinstein and Kroese 2011; Robert and Casella 2004).

An interesting extension of the analysis consists of relying on simulation methodologies for determining the relevant thresholds (namely, the risk tolerance threshold coupled with intermediate thresholds) which is one of the most promising applications of the probabilistic analysis.

Recall that the level of the Risk Profile is known since it is defined in advance. The level of the Risk Capacity is known (and exogenous for the intermediary) as well. At this regard, however, it is to note that the capacity could be defined by the supervisory authority (at least in part), taking into consideration (case by case) the design of the probabilistic distribution.

The tolerance threshold can be defined endogenously (before and after the buffer as determined by the board) together with the intermediate threshold.

More precisely, given the relevant parameter (for instance, the total capital ratio—TCR) and the risk appetite, the probabilistic analysis might lead to the definition of:

(a)  A Technical Risk Tolerance;
(b)  Intermediate thresholds;
(c)  Possibly, a buffer.

Risk tolerance represents the expected deviance (calculated on the basis of the expectations regarding the parameters of the forecasting model) for the relevant parameter. Contrary to other approaches the tolerance level is not defined on the basis of the absolute level of risk profile[2]; rather, it is determined in terms of the probability of not achieving the risk appetite level.

The intermediate threshold serves to the purpose of defining when deviations in the risk profile should be considered as significant, prompting organizational adjustments. Therefore, a probabilistic approach to RAF allows to properly assess the degree of challenge that a strategic plan involves and the underlying degree of risk (measured by the dispersion of outcomes).

Finally, an extra buffer (EB) can be deliberated by the board. While the technical risk tolerance represents the expected deviation, the extra buffer is intended to capture unexpected deviations from the expected scenario due to non-predictable events. Such an adjustment implies a shifting of the entire curve toward worsening scenarios.

## 6.3   Forecasting Models and Sensitivity Analysis: A Probabilistic Approach

As known, models offer a simplified representation of the real world designing a system of relations among variables. A model is defined by a set of input parameters, a set of target parameters and the mutual links. As inputs, a set of both exogenous variables and of endogenous variables is defined. Among exogenous variables, scenario variables (i.e. macroeconomic variables) such as inflation rates (which can affect certain cost items) or loan impairment rates could be included as well. For forecasting models to be reliable, they are required to take into account all available information. In fact, forecasts are subject to increasing stochastic errors with the time horizon they cover.

Given an appropriate number of stochastic simulations, it is possible to represent the arriving values for each scenario. More precisely, once having calibrated the model outputs based on scenario expected values and the goals that the bank want to pursue, aleatory features are then introduced.

We follow describe the steps of a simplified approach to probabilistic analysis for defining tolerance thresholds for a set of variables and, finally, gauging the boundaries for risk and performance measures.

Phase 1. Design of the forecasting model. It involves defining the target variables and, therefore, the input variables (environmental and strategic variables). Input variables can represent both the scenario and the strategy that the bank intends to pursue. For instance, let consider the Roe and the total capital ratio as target variables. Consider then one of the environmental variables (expected growth of the loan portfolio) as semi-endogenous. An adverse scenario should take into account lower loans given the target of profitability or higher loans given the risk target

**Table 6.1** The forecasting model

The budget constraint can be defined in a simplified way. Let the asset side comprising liquid assets (C) and illiquid loans (L), distinguishing between customers loans ((L*)) and loans to institutional counterparties (I). In the liability side, we have deposits (D) and equity (E). Within a T-period time horizon (generally, 3–5 years), the model has the goal of defining the better strategy (i.e. that allowing to realistically capture market opportunities while keeping the bank on track with both internal and supervisory constraints). The objective function is defined by Eq. 6.1 where it is assumed that the changes in equity capital only depend on the accumulation of profits ($U_t$).

$$\max(E_T); \text{con } E_T = E_0 + \sum_{t=1}^{T} U_t \quad (6.1)$$

Equation 6.2 restates the objective function and shows how the capital maximization is represented by the maximization of the overall contribution of profits within the forecasting period ($U_t$). Such an equation holds also when exogenous changes of capital are allowed ($E_T = E_0 + \sum_{t=1}^{T} U_t + \sum_{t=1}^{T} \Delta_t^E$).

$$\max\left(\sum_{t=1}^{T} U_t\right) = \sum_{\forall t=1..T} \max(U_t | U_{<t}) \quad (6.2)$$

The model is based on the identity assured by Eq. 6.3. It is to note that the profit in period t is not independent of the previous-years profits ($U_{<t}$).

$$U_t = U_t | U_{(<t)} = C_t + L_t^* + I_t - D_t - E_t^* t = 1\,T \quad (6.3)$$

$E_t^*$ equals $E_0 + \sum_1^{k-1} U_k$, or $E_0 + \sum_{k=1}^{t-1} U_k + \sum_{k=1}^{t} \Delta_k^E$ in the case exogenous features in variations of capital are introduced. It is to note that the profit of the period ($U_t$) is calculated on the basis of the profit account equation and that the balance is achieved through variations in institutional loans.

Let represent the relations that define the evolution of the model between subsequent forecasting periods. The functional relations assume that changes in total loans are due to loans coming to maturity $M^L$ and new loans $\Delta^L$. The intertemporal relations for deposits can be defined in the same way.

$$L_{t+1} = L_t - M_{t+1}^L + \Delta t + 1^L \forall t = 1..T \quad (6.4)$$

For the sake of simplicity, among those loans coming to maturity defaulted loans can be included as well with weight $\delta^M$ on total matured loans. Equation (6.5) proposes the intertemporal relation for capital[3] ($r_\delta$ represents provisions).

$$E_{t+1} = E_t + r_L * L_{t+1} - r_D * D_{t+1} - r_\delta * \delta_{t+1}^L * M_{t+1}^L \quad (6.5)$$

Putting aside $E_t$, the other terms on the right side of the equation provide a simplified representation of the profit for the year (as from the profit and loss account).

Equation 6.5 assumes that the average returns on loans and deposits are time invariant. Such a hypothesis could be easily overcome using interest rates coherent with the strategy that the bank wants to pursue.

(continued)

**Table 6.1** (continued)

The model results are, then, employed in order to assess the risks (credit risk, operational risk, interest rate risk and so on). Supervisory or internal limits become a constraint within the deterministic setting of the model. The probabilistic analysis is aimed at determining and assessing the risk that both the evolution of scenarios and the bank strategy will lead to a breach of them.

alternatively. Provided that such conflicts when defining the adverse scenario refer to $k$ target variables (each assuming, for instance, two values), the number of unfavourable scenarios to be considered would be $2^k$. Table 6.1 offers a simplified representation of the forecasting model.

Phase 2. Assessing the deviation of scenarios from the expected scenario. This step leads to the estimation of variation ranges for the input variables, which, together with their expected values, allows to derive a distribution probability (Phase 3).

Phase 3. Designing the stochastic structure of the forecasting model. This step leads to deriving the probability distributions assumed as independent at this stage. Moreover, correlations between marginal distributions are derived, either relying on estimations based on time series analysis or recurring to experts' elicitations.

To this end, copula-based risk analysis allows to map correlations between the model's aleatory variables.

Moreover, a probabilistic analysis allows certain degrees of flexibility by introducing "sampling rules" in order to define the domain within which variables can be jointly sampled. At this regard, it is worth noting that the copula approach often offers solutions which are just an approximation to the problem of sampling values from multivariate joint distributions where correlations are different from zero. It is therefore possible to sample values related to very rare and unlikely scenarios. Defining proper sampling rules elicits therefore "coherence checks", accepting or refusing unlikely scenarios.

After having identified the parameters representing the envisaged scenarios, a probability function which describes uncertainty is required. For instance, let $X$ be a generic parameter of the model and $\dddot{X} = \{x \in (x_l, x_u) : P(x) \neq 0\}^4$ the related domain, we can define a probability distribution $[f(x)]$ on the domain so that it satisfies the following conditions $\int_{x_l}^{x_u} f(t)\mathrm{dt} = 1$; and $P(x_l \leq a \leq x \leq b \leq x_u) = \int_a^b f(t)\,\mathrm{dt}$. A *BETA* distribution is normally applied to describe the stochastic structure of the variables in the model. However, for the purpose of representing the variability of input variables, a *PERT* distribution can be applied as well (O'Hagan 2006).

Phase 4. Derivation and analysis of results. Simulations allow to empirically derive the distribution probabilities of target variables. Such probabilities are conditional on the specific model and the hypothesis over the input variables.

Hereafter, we describe, in practical terms, the rationale for the application of a probabilistic approach to RAF thresholds. Let consider the total capital ratio (TRC—that, as known, reflects the ratio supervisory capital and the risk weighted assets—RWA) as the output parameter, although we might well assume other parameters as outputs in a probabilistic forecasting model. Such a parameter is, by construction, negatively correlated to risk.

Figure 6.1 depicts a hypothetical distribution of the output parameter. Let assume a Risk Appetite (RA) greater than the Risk Profile (RP) with both above the Risk Capacity (RC).

Of paramount importance is the interpretation of the areas P(TCR < risk capacity) and P(TCR) > risk appetite), denoted with A and D respectively. Each of the four areas in Fig. 6.5 have a significant economic meaning. In particular:

(a)  The first area (A) represents, when different to zero, the probability that TCR is lower than the risk capacity. It defines an "absolute risk" measure, being the probability of not complying with the minimum regulatory capital requirement;

(b)  Area B in the figure (when different to zero) identifies the probability that TCR is lower than the risk profile. It defines a "relative risk" measure, being the probability of obtaining a capital level below the current capitalization;

(c)  Area C in the figure above (necessarily different to zero), identifies the probability that TCR is lower than the risk appetite but higher than the risk profile. It is the probability of improving the current situation but still remaining below the target levels;

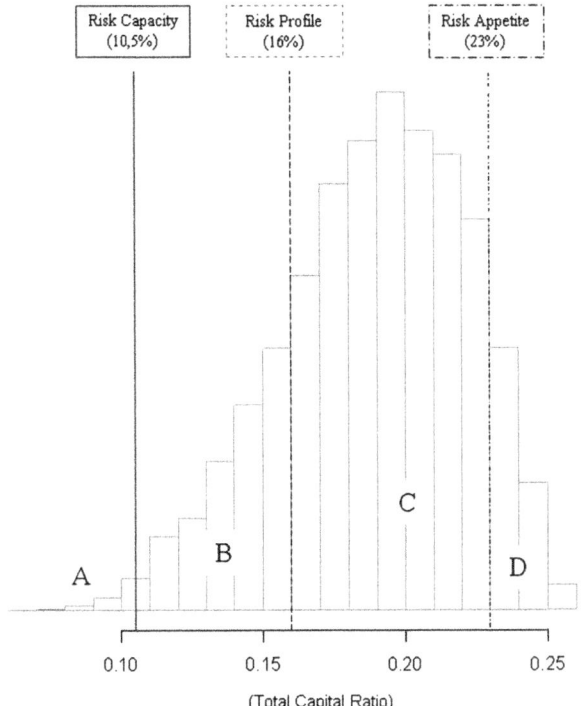

**Fig. 6.1** Total capital ratio distribution, an example

(d) Area D in the figure above (necessarily different from zero) identify the probability that TCR is greater than the risk appetite. Such a probability is inversely related to the degree of the challenge implied by the plan. Higher values of such a probability mean that improving scenarios are easily achievable (low degree of challenge).

As noted, the RAF emerges as a powerful tool for strategic planning processes. It allows to set risk-return targets characterized by different degrees of challenge, monitor the achievements and assess the feasibility of the plan.

Obviously, different shapes of the distribution coupled with varying risk appetites result in different absolute-risk exposures.

*I° case. Very challenging and highly risky plan.*

*Possible exposure to absolute risk-inability to*

*comply with the risk capacity*

*I° case. Moderately challenging and highly risky*

*plan. Possible exposure to absolute risk-inability to*

*comply with the risk capacity*

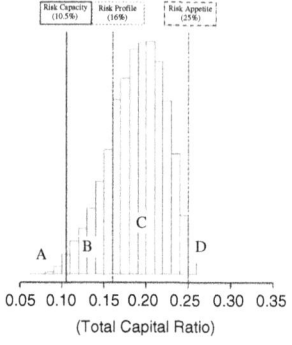

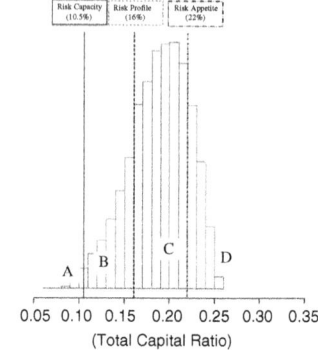

**Fig. 6.2**   TCR probability distribution in a high absolute risk environment

Let us consider the absolute-risk environments depicted in Figs. 6.2 and 6.3, which represent different combinations of challenge and riskiness of the plan.

The left-hand side in Fig. 6.4 is referred to a bank operating within an absolute risk framework (positive probability that *TCR < risk capacity*). It builds a very challenging (very low probability that *TCR > risk appetite)* and therefore probably unrealistic plan. In the second case (right hand side of the picture), while the shape of the curve remains the same, the strategic framework changes defining a less challenging plan.

Let note that in both cases the probability distribution has a median value very close to the risk profile. Such a feature is due to casualty here and does not constitute a rule. Figure 6.5 depicts two cases of limited risk exposure, the probability of breaching the risk capacity and different degree of challenge.

Within a zero-absolute-risk environment, Case III represents the case of a bank pursuing relatively low challenging goals (in no scenarios, we have TCR > risk capacity), which are not affected by the combined effect of exogenous forces and uncertainties related to the achievement of endogenous targets. In case IV, the strategic plan benefits of a

I Case. Less challenging and less risky plan (absolute risk null)

II Case. Highly challenging but conservative plan (absolute risk exposure null)

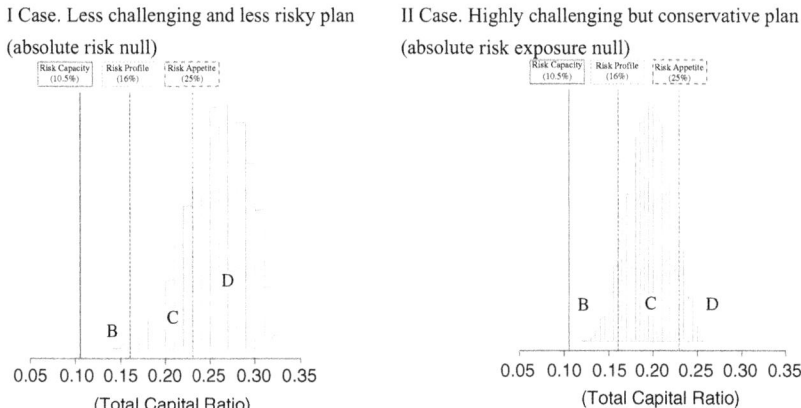

**Fig. 6.3** TCR probability distribution within a zero absolute risk environment

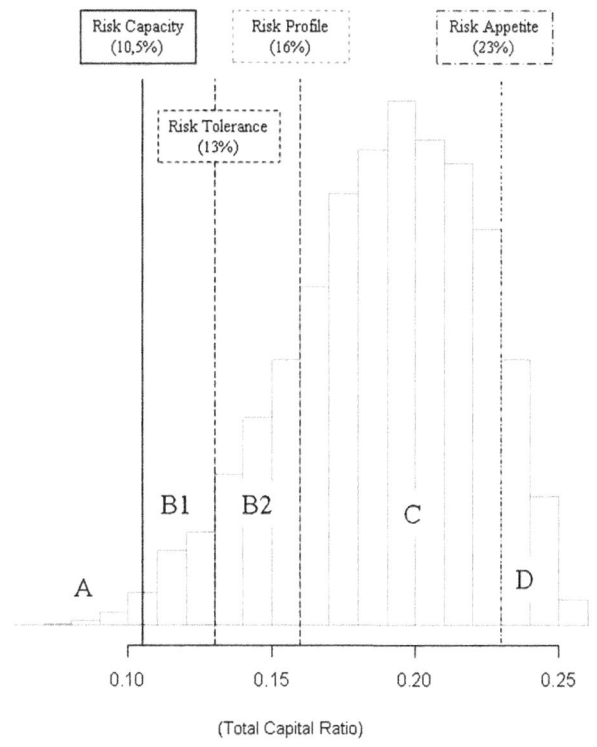

**Fig. 6.4** Introducing thresholds

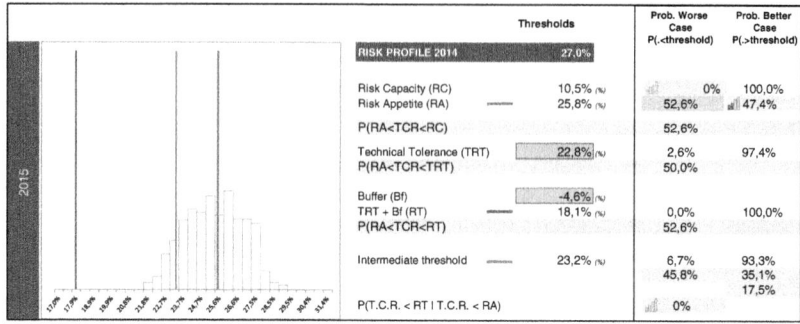

**Fig. 6.5** A synthesis of RAF thresholds: the total capital ratio

negligible absolute-risk exposure while having a very challenging TCR target.

When introducing thresholds, the B area in Fig. 6.4 identifies the probability that TCR takes lower than the risk tolerance values (assuming that such a parameter is lower than both risk appetite and risk profile: $P(TCR < RT \mid TCR < RA)$) and mirrors a most accurate and conservative relative risk measure. In a case of worse than expected performance, such a value signals the probability that the performance itself be worse than the corporate threshold (risk tolerance) that has been defined within the RAF procedure.

More generally, a possible methodological approach, on the basis of the sensitivity analysis (starting from an exogenously defined risk capacity), defines the thresholds as follows:

(a)  The risk appetite is determined as the result of the forecasting model in its first deterministic version;
(b)  The degree of the Technical Risk Tolerance (TRT) (i.e. deriving from a probabilistic assessment without Buffer) can be identified by properly defining the area $(C + D; (P(TRT < TCR < RA))$ assuming that the probability of achieving lower than the risk appetite values (but greater than the risk tolerance) is lower than a conventional threshold (for example, 50%). More generally, the technical tolerance can be identified with the point at which $P(TRT < TCR < RA) = MIN(C + D; 50\%).$[5]

(c) The board can deliberate an extra buffer. In a simplified approach, the extra buffer might, for example, be defined as a function of the volatility of the parameter (conventionally, it is measured as 3 standard deviations of the parameter distribution).

(d) Intermediate threshold (IT). Within a simplified approach it could be conventionally located between the risk appetite and the risk tolerance gross of the possible buffer (for example, 1/3 of such a distance expressed in terms of width of such an interval or, alternatively, following a probability approach: $P(SI < TCR < RA) = \frac{1}{3} * P(RT < TCR < RA))$.

Apart from the specific methodological choices, the fundamental point is that the thresholds are defined on the basis of the information which directly derive from probabilistic simulations and are strictly related to the strategic planning.

## 6.4   Probabilistic Analysis: A Simulation

The results of the stochastic forecasting analysis are themselves expressed in terms of probability distribution.

Let consider as an exemplification the Return on Equity (ROE) and the Total Capital Ratio (TCR) as target parameters. They are for sure representative of fundamental profiles of bank management (overall profitability and degree of riskiness). They are obviously interdependent.

We present examples of marginal distribution probabilities for the ROE and TCR taking 2015 as the reference year with reference to projections made in 2014 in the following. Figure 6.5 depicts the distribution for the TCR showing:

(a) The histogram of simulations that represents the marginal distribution probability of the parameter, evidencing the relevant thresholds (left-hand quadrant);

(b) The values of the most significant thresholds (in the middle);

(c) The probability of achieving better or worse results than the thresholds (right-hand side quadrant).

The risk profile is the value of the parameter in 2014. It is determined based on historical data and helps interpreting the expected dynamics. Risk capacity (defined by regulators) was 10.5% (assumed invariant over years). From Fig. 6.5, we learn that:

(a) The bank is well capitalized and not exposed to absolute risk (Prob(TCR < capacity) = 0);
(b) The risk appetite is located at the median level of the distribution;
(c) The technical risk tolerance is set in such way to have a 50% probability of achieving values comprised between the risk tolerance and the risk appetite;
(d) The buffer (defined by the board) makes a 4.6% translation of the technical tolerance bringing the tolerance to an 18.1% level;
(e) The intermediate threshold is set at a one-third level of the distance between risk appetite and risk tolerance (comprising the buffer). It emerges that in 93.3% of the cases TCR lays above the intermediate threshold.

With reference to the ROE (Fig. 6.6), we can raise the following points:

(a) Obviously, a risk capacity does not exist. However, it could be assumed that the cost of capital (KE) acts as the capacity for that parameter. Below such a threshold, in fact, the economic value added (EVA) is negative (ROE < KE) thus destroying the value for shareholders;
(b) The bank forecasts (the Risk Appetite) a negative return (−0.7%). However, 78% of the scenarios point to better than expected results;
(c) The technical tolerance lays at the limits of expected results (probability of lower values = 1.9%), while the buffer defined by the board returns an intermediate threshold equal to −1.4% (probability of achieving lower values = 0%).

For the sake of completeness, Table 6.2 summarizes the RAF parameters for which, in our exercise, we calculated the risk appetite together with risk tolerance and risk tolerance thresholds according to the probabilistic approach.

**Table 6.2**  A list of RAF parameters and thresholds as defined with a probabilistic approach (2015)

| Risk parameter | Risk capacity | Risk tolerance (%) | Intermediate risk threshold (%) | Risk appetite (%) |
|---|---|---|---|---|
| Total capital ratio | 10,50% | 18.15 | 23.22 | 25.75 |
| Total internal capital/Total capital | – | 0.00 | 0.00 | 46.90 |
| ROE (evaluated on an average level of own funds over the last 2 years) | – | −3.02 | −1.45 | −0.66 |
| Adjusted Cost/Income (net of the outcomes of the financial area) | – | 85.07 | 81.56 | 79.81 |
| Own funds/Total assets | – | 9.51 | 12.82 | 14.48 |
| Gross customer loans/funding vs customers | – | 122.64 | 103.75 | 94.31 |
| Capital requirement for credit risk/Own funds | – | 36.77 | 30.47 | 27.32 |
| (Non-performing loans)/Own funds | – | 62.96 | 56.39 | 53.10 |
| Coverage ratio | – | 63.07 | 64.05 | 64.54 |
| Exposure to the top 20 customers/Total gross loans | – | 21.88 | 21.48 | 21.28 |
| Internal capital on interest rate risk/Own Funds | – | 20.61 | 16.85 | 14.97 |

The estimates (available for each year under investigation) are proposed for 2015 only (strategic plan for 2014). For parameter and for each forecasting year, a synthesis of the thresholds resembling those in Figs. 6.5 and 6.6 is available.

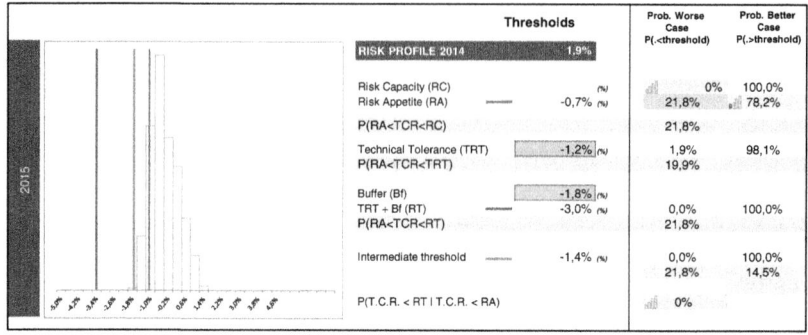

**Fig. 6.6** A synthesis of RAF thresholds: the ROE

We then propose a further possible application of the model for the purpose of implementing a monitoring tool for certain parameters which can be assumed as representing operational limits within the planning process.

In such a perspective, the commercial budget on funding (D) and loans (L) certainly is one of the fundamental tools for deterministic forecasting, probabilistic analysis and the definition of RAF thresholds.

A question that could be useful to raise is as follows: What are the limits up to which it is possible to fail the target volumes for loans (L) and deposits (D) while assuring compliance with RAF thresholds? The problem is, therefore, to define the conditional distribution of the variables in relation to the constraint that has been imposed under the RAF approach (e.g., the intermediate threshold referred to ROE and TCR). More precisely, we can define the distributions of loans and deposits conditioned to the compliance with the intermediate thresholds for ROE and TCR. Formally:

$$P(D \mid ROE > -1.45\%; TCR > 23.22\%); \ P(L \mid ROE > -1.45\%; TCR > 23.22\%)$$

Given the distribution of loans and deposits, it is, then, possible do break it down in order to identify buckets representing different degrees of the risk of not complying with intermediate thresholds. At this regard, it is possible to represent different risk scenarios and namely:

(a) High-risk scenarios represented by values outside the curve, corresponding to the (certain) failure to comply with strategic guidelines (high probability of breaching the intermediate threshold);
(b) Low-risk scenarios which, conventionally, can be identified within a range of $\pm 1$ standard deviation from the mean (but never outside the curve);
(c) Moderate-risk scenarios, in all the other cases when intermediate risk thresholds are identified.

The monitoring tool allows to compare budgetary figures for loans and deposits with current volumes as reported.

## 6.5 Conclusions

Forecasting processes in banking institutions require the support of appropriate models for decision-making. Projecting and assessing risk exposure, therefore, do not constitute a mere consequence of financial planning, rather is a constitutional part of it. Under such a perspective, our work explored the application of a probabilistic forecasting model for the purpose of defining the RAF thresholds. The outcomes are conditioned to the structure of the model and to the strategic guidelines that have been implemented.

The model measures what would happen when, under a probabilistic scenario, the projected strategies would be implemented assuming the validity of the forecasting model itself.

The Bank of Italy points to the need of carrying on stress tests with the aim of assessing the impacts of unfavourable scenarios. The definition of RAF thresholds can, therefore, be implemented in the analysis of worst-than-planned scenarios.

In such a perspective, *stress test* can be defined in terms of a sensitivity analysis of the model to the starting hypothesis. Within this framework, thresholds are no longer defined in an exogenous way. Nor they are determined as a function of the risk appetite only, independent of the probabilistic distribution of outcomes. Finally, the probabilistic approach we proposed is just not a tool for pursuing a single specific technical goal. Rather, it qualifies as a tool for supporting bank governance which, as known, is based on probability intervals. In that, it tends to investigate the sensitivity of the outcomes of a forecasting model to the underlying hypothesis taking the stochastic nature of events into consideration.

# Notes

1. For the links between corporate governance and shareholder wealth, see Shleifer and Vishny (1997). For a great review of general corporate governance principles in banking institutions, see Mehran et al. (2011); Mehran and Mollineaux (2012).
2. Formally: Upper (lower) Risk Tolerance $= \mu$ risk profile $+(-)$ m $\times$ $\sigma$ risk profile; upper (lower) risk limit $= \mu$ risk profile $+(-)$ l $\times$ $\sigma$ risk profile, where m and l are the multipliers of the volatility.
3. The maximum amount of new deposits from (and new loans to) customers (and therefore the definition of a minimum and maximum value for the loans-to-deposits ratio) represents a fundamental constraint given that for a medium–small bank institutional funding sources are limited.
4. Where x is a generic value of the parameter X, P(x) denotes the probability associated with the generic value x, x_l and x_u are the lower and the upper limit of the domain, respectively.
5. In the case of a strategic plan with a medium–high degree of challenge (C + D > 50%), it is conventionally assumed that the probabilistic distance between RT and RA is 50%. By contrast, in the case of a strategic plan with a medium–low degree of challenge, RT is set to the maximum distance to RA taking into account the distribution probability of the parameter. The rationale for choosing a 50% cut-off is to preserve a degree of elasticity between RT and RA so that for the most challenging plans the breach of a warning threshold (RT or intermediate) promptly alerts the bodies entrusted with controlling responsibilities. By contrast, a plan, which is already characterized by a low level of challenge, will lead to the definition of an RT levels that even more promptly generate warnings.

# References

Alix, M., S. Venkat, Z. Mogul, S. Leung, M. Banks, and J. Saary Littman. 2015. Risk appetite frameworks: Insights into evolving global practices. *Global Credit Review* 5: 1–17.

Baldan, C., E. Geretto, and F. Zen. 2014. Managing banking risk with the risk appetite framework: A quantitative model for the Italian banking system. *MPRA Paper*, 59504.

Baldan, C., E. Geretto, and F. Zen. 2016. A quantitative model to articulate the banking risk appetite framework. *Journal of Risk Management in Financial Institutions* 9 (2): 175–196.

Basel Committee on Banking Supervision. 2009. Proposed enhancements to the Basel II framework. *Bank for International Settlements*.

Basel Committee on Banking Supervision. 2013. Principles for effective risk data aggregation and risk reporting. *Bank for International Settlements*, Basel. http://www.bis.org/publ/bcbs239.pdf.

Booz&Co. 2009. *A comprehensive risk appetite frameworks for banks*. New York: Booz&Co.

Central Bank of Ireland. 2014. *Risk appetite*. A discussion paper, Dublin.

Committee of European Banking Supervision. 2010. High level principles for risk management, February.

Cortez, A. 2011. *Winning at risk*. Hoboken: Wiley Finance.

Cremonino, A. 2011. Risk appetite as a core element of ERM: Definition and process, Enterprise risk management symposium. *Society of Actuaries*.

Counterparty Risk Management Policy Group. 2008. Containing systemic risk: The road to reform, The Report of the CRMPG III.

ECRS—EMEA Centre for Regulatory Strategy. 2013. Risk appetite framework. How to spot the genuine article. Deloitte, July.

Financial Stability Board. 2013a. Thematic review on risk governance. Peer Review Report.

Financial Stability Board. 2013b. Principles for an effective risk appetite framework.

Fernandes, K.J., A.D. Grody, P.J. Hughes, O. Phillips, and J.S. Toms. 2013. Risk accounting: An accounting based approach to measuring enterprise risk and risk appetite: 28–33. http://ssrn.com/abstract=2165034abstract = 2165034.

Global Association of Risk Professional Risk Appetite Framework Challenge, December 2013.

Grody, A.D., and P.J. Hughes. 2016. Risk accounting—Part 1: The risk data aggregation and risk reporting (BCBS 239) foundation of enterprise risk management (ERM) and risk governance. *Journal of Risk Management in Financial Institutions* 9 (2): 130–146.

Institute of International Finance. 2011. Implementing robust risk appetite Frameworks to strengthen financial institutions. Washington, June.

K.P.M.G. 2013. Developing a Strong Risk Appetite Program. Challenges and solutions. https://assets.kpmg.com/content/dam/kpmg/pdf/2013/11/risk-appetite-v2.pdf.

McNish, R., A. Schlosser, F. Selandari, U. Stegemann, and J. Vorholt. 2013. Getting to ERM. A road map for banks and other financial institutions (McKinsey Working Paper series on risk, 43).

Mehran, H., A. Morrison, and J. Shapiro. 2011. Corporate governance and banks: What have we learned from the financial crisis? Federal Reserve Bank of New York Staff Reports, 502, June.

Mehran, H., and L. Mollineaux. 2012. Corporate governance of financial institutions. Federal Reserve Bank of New York Staff Reports, 539, January.

O'Hagan, A. 2006. *Uncertain judgements: Eliciting experts' probabilities*. Wiley.

Protiviti. 2012. Defining risk appetite. Early mover series. https://www.protiviti.com/sites/default/files/united_states/pov-defining-risk-appetite-protiviti.pdf.

Risk and Insurance Management Society. 2012. Exploring risk appetite and risk tolerance. https://www.rims.org/resources/ERM/Documents/RIMS_Exploring_Risk_Appetite_Risk_Tolerance_0412.pdf.

Robert, C.P., and G. Casella. 2004. *Monte carlo statistical methods*. Springer Texts in Statistics. New York.

Rubinstein, R.Y., and D.P. Kroese. 2011. *Simulation and the Monte Carlo method*. New York: Wiley.

Shleifer, A., and R.W. Vishny. 1997. A survey of corporate governance. *Journal of Finance* 52 (2): 737–783.

Stulz, R.M. 2016. Risk management, governance, culture and risk taking in banks. *FRBNY Economic Policy Review*, August.

Senior Supervisors Group. 2010. Observations on developments in risk appetite framework and IT infrastructure, December.

The Institute of Risk Management. 2011. Risk appetite & tolerance. Guidance paper, September.

The Society of Actuaries in Ireland. 2011. Constructing a risk appetite framework: An introduction, Dublin.

# Authors' Biography

**Maurizio Polato** is full professor in Banking and Finance in Udine University. His research fields mainly relate to the securities and exchange industry and bank performance. He is author of various publications on the topic which address issues related to the industry structure, measurement of performances and value for securities exchanges and regulation.

**Josanco Floreani** is Associate Professor in Corporate Finance in the Department of Economics and Statistics, University of Udine. He graduated in Economics at the University of Udine, where he also received his Ph.D. His main research interests are related to firm's financial performances and governance and Islamic Finance.

**Giuseppe Giannelli** born in 1971, has been working in Federazione delle BCC di Puglia e Basilicata since January 2008. He got a degree Economics (University of Bari, 1996) and a post-degree MBA (Profingest—Almaweb). He also worked at Prometeia—Bologna as an analyst of banks before and as a consultant in strategic planning.

**Nicola Novielli** born in 1981, has been working in Federazione delle BCC di Puglia e Basilicata since March 2012. He got a Degree in Statistics and Economics (University of Bari—2005), a Master in Medical Statistics (University of Leicester, UK, 2008) and a Ph.D. in Health Economics (University of Leicester, UK, 2010). He worked at the University of Birmingham from July 2010 to February 2012 at the Public Health Department.

# 7

# The Determinants of CDS Spreads: The Case of Banks

Maria Mazzuca, Caterina Di Tommaso and Fabio Piluso

## 7.1 Introduction

Credit Default Swaps (CDS) are credit derivatives functioning as insurance contracts: in exchange for a fee paid to the seller, they provide protection to buyers from losses that may be incurred on sovereign or corporate debt resulting from a credit event that may include failure to pay (interest or principal on) and restructuring (of one or more obligations issued by the sovereign or the corporate) (IMF 2013). What makes the difference between a CDS and an insurance contract is that CDS contracts are freely tradable while insurance contracts are not.

CDS market became very significant in terms of volume during the last years, although its values dropped considerably during the financial crisis, mostly due to the investors' concerns about the fact that they are unregulated to a large extent as they are part of the over-the-counter

M. Mazzuca (✉) · C. Di Tommaso · F. Piluso
University of Calabria, Rende, Italy
e-mail: maria.mazzuca@unical.it

© The Author(s) 2017

G. Chesini et al. (eds.), *Financial Markets, SME Financing and Emerging Economies*,
Palgrave Macmillan Studies in Banking and Financial Institutions,
DOI 10.1007/978-3-319-54891-3_7

(OTC) market. However, the CDS market remains sizeable, dominated by institutional investors (insurance companies and, more recently, hedge funds) and banks (Augustin et al. 2014).

The market evolution of CDS is intimately related to banks because they are the main originators of credit risk. Moreover, it seems that some trends in lending activity and in banks' risk-taking behaviour can influence the CDS market volume; for instance, it can be observed that as a consequence of the fact that large firms tend to gradually reduce the number of banking relationships, banks could tend to take on more risk that, in turn, they try to reduce by transferring it to third parties using credit derivatives.

The literature on CDS in banks has mainly focused on the potential effects of the use of CDS by banks—hedging versus speculative instruments (e.g. Minton et al. 2009). In this paper, the focus is on banks, but we use a perspective different than the one generally found in the previous literature. We are interested in studying CDS of banks as signals of their soundness and their risk of insolvency. In fact, CDS spreads should reflect market perceptions about the financial health of banks and can be used by regulators to extract warning signals regarding the financial stability (Annaert et al. 2013).

Studying CDS spreads determinants in banks is interesting for a number of reasons. First, because banks are important players on this market but have a special nature compared to other types of firms, due to the heavy regulation to which they are subjected, the high leverage, their special assets and trading activities that may create uncertainty and agency problems (Raunig and Scheicher 2009). As a consequence, the investors' perceptions and judgement of credit risk could be influenced by factors different than those typically considered to be important for other firms. Second, banks play an important role in financial systems. Since banks are strictly interconnected to each other, an increase in a bank's risk or the bank's default can produce important spillovers and, in crisis periods, contagion (e.g. European Commission 2014). Systemic risk caused by a default of a bank is so dangerous that the prudential authorities proceeded to further regulate the risk-taking behaviour of banks (Basel 3) by tightening the existing rules (such as those on capital requirements) and by introducing new prudential rules (such as liquidity ratios).

Since the 2007/2008 financial crisis mainly affected financial institutions, it is interesting to focus on them to better understand the mechanism by which the market assesses the risk of these special firms by pricing the CDS. Third, banks are important agents in every economic system and the insolvency of a bank has a very strong interconnection with the economy of a country. Even though a default of a bank can affect the economy through different channels, the main concern is related to the potentially dangerous effects on loans (volume and pricing) and on deposits. In some areas, such as Europe, this concern has recently been amplified by the new tightened rules on banks' recovery and resolution[1] (that implies the bail-in mechanism) that, among others, specify the sequence in which the power to write down or convert liabilities in resolution should be applied.

Despite the important role that financial intermediaries play on this market, little work exists regarding CDS spreads in the banking sector. One reason could be that the financial industry is considered to be an opaque industry where traditional credit risk models are likely to be less successful (Annaert et al. 2013). This could find confirmation in the fact that variables that proved to be significant determinants of credit spreads of non-financial companies tend to lose their explanatory power when applied to financial companies (Boss and Scheicher 2005; Raunig and Scheicher 2009). Another hypothesis is that for banks, other risk indicators are available and are considered important, such as the Basel capital ratios.

This study aims at offering several contributions to the literature. First, it enriches the literature focused on the banks' CDS spreads and it aims to increase the understanding of the determinants of CDS premium in this very special and relevant sector. Additionally, we want to investigate more deeply the credit spread puzzle issues that in the context of banks could be more pronounced and more challenging to address with respect to other types of firms (Hasan et al. 2015). Second, our research extends the previous studies both in terms of coverage of the sample and in terms of depth of analysis. Our sample is composed of international banks, while samples of other previous studies include banks that are active in more narrow geographical areas (Annaert et al. 2013, Kanagaretnam et al. 2016). Third, the debate on the role of CDS in the stability of financial systems is still ongoing (IMF 2013). CDS can be viewed as useful market-based risk indicators and valuable hedging instruments or as speculative tools suggesting that their prices do not reflect underlying fundamentals or actual risks, therefore unduly raising funding costs for governments (and corporations), threatening fiscal sustainability and exacerbating market tensions. The role of CDS for the financial stability is particularly important when banks are considered.

We study the determinants of CDS spreads using a regression analysis and focusing on a sample of 86 international banks from 2009 to 2012. We find the following main results. The explanatory power of the model increases when bank-specific and market/country variables are considered. Banks' capitalisation, size and rating are significant determinants of CDS spread. Among market factors, the market volatility and the slope of the yield curve prove to affect the CDS spread.

The remainder of the paper is organised as follows. In Sect. 7.2, we discuss the relevant literature. In Sect. 7.3, we describe the methodology and the data. In Sect. 7.4, we analyse the variables used in our models. In Sect. 7.5, we present and discuss the empirical analysis and its results. In Sect. 7.6, we discuss the results of the robustness tests. Finally, in Sect. 7.7, we summarise and conclude.

## 7.2    Literature

### 7.2.1  Studies on (Bonds and) CDS Spreads

Since CDS are relatively new products, literature about CDS spreads relies on the literature regarding credit spreads of corporate bonds. The theoretical literature on the determinants of credit spreads relies on Merton's seminal paper (1974). According to the credit risk theory deriving from Merton's model, the credit spreads depend on four (structural) factors: the risk-free interest rate, the level of the firm's debt (face value), the market value of the firm and the volatility of the firm's assets. Merton's theory is accepted by academics, but empirical studies following the theory generally do not confirm that structural default factors are able to sufficiently explain the credit spreads of bonds[2] (credit spread puzzle). As a consequence, the previous literature identifies several other factors, different than structural credit risk factors, helping to explain the credit spread changes (such as a non-diversifiable credit risk/systematic risk, a liquidity premium, several market-wide variables, different firm-specific factors) (Driessen 2005; Amato and Remolona 2003; Collin-Dufresne et al. 2001; Elton et al. 2001).

Only during the last decade, the literature started focusing directly on CDS spreads (rather than on bond spreads). Their relevance is due to the fact that they are representative of important structural developments in financial markets (Boss and Scheicher 2005). Furthermore, it is generally recognised that CDS allow studying credit spreads (O'Kane and Sen 2005) better than bonds for several reasons. First, CDS are directly observable, while bond spreads have to be derived by comparing corporate bonds to a risk-free asset that could imply problems when the choice has to be done (Annaert et al. 2013). Moreover, they can be considered fairly pure indicators of credit risk because the structure separates the credit risk component from other risks, such as interest rate and currency risk (FitchRatings 2007). Second, they are "light" instruments in that one does not need to fund an entire bond position, for example, to have essentially identical credit risk exposure (FitchRatings 2007). Third, bond spreads are more prone to be affected by several factors, such as market and institutional factors (liquidity, tax effects and market microstructure effects) (Annaert et al. 2013). Fourth, given their derivative nature, CDS spreads are more efficient and more rapid than bonds in signalling changes in the credit quality of the borrowers so that their power in price discovery process is more efficient (e.g. Carboni 2011; Coudert and Gex 2010; Ammer and Cai 2011; Blanco et al. 2005; Aktung et al. 2009). This last advantage of the CDS is confirmed by the importance which CDS assumed during the recent financial turmoil when regulators also started to focus on financial markets information and signals to take their policy actions.

The literature on CDS spreads can be virtually divided into studies focused on sovereign CDS (Fontana and Scheicher 2010; Heinz and Sun 2014; Drago and Gallo 2016) and those focused on (financial or non-financial) corporate CDS (e.g. Di Cesare and Guazzarotti 2010; Zhang et al. 2009). Given the objectives of the present work, we are interested in empirical studies focused on financial institutions' CDS. This literature includes a rather limited number of studies.

Düllmann and Sosinska (2007) consider three German banks during the period 2002–2005. They analyse CDS spreads focusing on the explanatory power of three risk sources: idiosyncratic credit risk, systematic credit risk and liquidity risk. They show that structural models based on equity prices and reduced-form models based on the prices of credit derivatives have their specific advantages and that together they can provide a more comprehensive assessment of the riskiness of the monitored banks.

Raunig and Scheicher (2009) compare 41 major banks to 162 non-banks during the period of 2003–2007. They investigate the determinants of CDS premium and, by means of regression analysis, they study how CDS investors discriminate between banks and non-banks and how their assessment has varied over time. They show that average CDS premium of banks is lower than non-banks' premium over the entire period and that the difference in the premium disappears during the turmoil. In their model, the empirical default probability (EDF is obtained from KMV database and represents an estimate of the probability of default based on the model of Merton), plus a vector of control variables (risk-free interest rate, slope of the yield curve, implied stock market volatility, idiosyncratic equity volatility, swap spread), is considered. They show that risk premium differs across time and across banks and non-banks and that the risk-free rate, implied stock market volatility and idiosyncratic volatility affect banks' CDS only to a small extent in the period from 10/2003 to 6/2007. During the turmoil (second semester of 2007), the significant determinants of banks' CDS tend to be the same for banks and non-banks with the exception of the slope of the yield curve that loses its explanatory power for banks. During the subprime turmoil, there exists a substantial repricing of banks' CDS relative to the CDS of other firms because banks have large exposures to securitisation instruments.

Annaert et al. (2013) study the determinants of (32) European listed banks CDS spreads during the period 2004–2010. They consider three sets of variables: credit risk variables (derived from the Merton's model), liquidity variables and market-wide factors. Their analysis confirms that the variables affecting CDS spreads vary across time (but not so much across rating classes). After the start of the crisis, structural factors gain significance, while bank-specific liquidity maintains its importance before and after the crisis. Some variables proxying the general economic conditions are important, but their significance and signs changed with the start of the crisis.

Hasan et al. (2015) study the determinants of (161) banks' CDS spreads from 23 countries during the period 2001–2011. They focus on three groups of variables: structural model variables, CAMELS factors,[3] and country-level, economic, governance and regulation factors. They show that some structural factors (leverage measures, equity return volatility and government bond yield) are significant determinants of banks' credit risk but that they have a limited explanation power (20%). CAMELS indicators provide incremental explanatory power (+10%). Asset quality (loan-loss provisions to total loans) is the most significant determinant of banks' CDS spreads (after controlling for time and bank fixed effects). Furthermore, they show that systematic risk and risk aversion (proxied by stock market return) are important determinants of CDS spreads. In addition, some country-level factors are significant because they influence the risk-taking behaviour of the banks: financial conglomerate restriction is negatively related to banks' CDS spreads (implying that competition helps to reduce the bank's credit risk), and deposit insurance is positively related to CDS spreads. Finally, since with time and bank fixed effects the model reaches 60–80%, they show that cross-bank variations in systematic risk and some unobserved time-varying factors have important explanatory power for banks' CDS spreads. During the crisis, the impacts of leverage and asset quality on CDS spreads become much stronger.

Kanagaretnam et al. (2016) analyse the determinants of 27 US Bank Holding Corporations (BHCs) for the 2001–2008 period and find that CDS spread is significantly associated with several CAMELS measures; their results indicate that BHCs with lower earnings and lower liquidity tend to have higher CDS spread. The study also demonstrates that risky ABS securities are an important driver of risk since 2006. In particular, their results indicate that BHCs with higher ABS balances are riskier and have a higher CDS spread. They also demonstrate that

CDS spread is positively and significantly associated with single-family (1–4 people) residential loans. Their results confirm that the real estate risk was a major risk for US BHCs during the financial crisis. Finally, they document that CDS spread is only significantly associated with equity market-based bank risk measures, but bears no association with other accounting-based bank risk measures, such as the standard deviation of historical return on asset, the standard deviation of historical net interest margin and Z-score. Consistent with Hasan et al. (2015), Liu et al. (2016) find that banks in countries with explicit deposit insurance systems have higher CDS spreads, supporting the "moral hazard" view. Explicit deposit insurance systems are positively and significantly related to bank CDS spreads for the 3-year, 5-year and 10-year periods, reflecting the "moral hazard" problem. Deposit insurance plays a stabilisation role when and where the market is volatile, as evidenced during the financial crisis and in countries with greater market volatility. This is consistent with the view that in the midst of a crisis, the immediate task is to restore confidence, and guarantees can be helpful.

Different from previous studies that fundamentally rely on the model of Merton (1974), Chiaramonte and Casu (2013) focus on balance-sheet indicators, suggesting that in the periods of financial stress, market data fluctuate wildly and changes in market data during a crisis period do not necessarily reflect the changes in credit risk. They investigate the determinants of CDS spreads and whether CDS spreads can be considered a good proxy of bank performance during the period 2005–2011. Their sample includes 57 international banks. They show that the determinants of CDS spreads vary across time. They demonstrate that banks' CDS spreads reflect the risk captured by the banks' balance-sheet ratios; the relationship between banks' CDS spreads and balance-sheet ratios becomes stronger during the crisis and post-crisis period; variables that a priori would be considered as determinants of CDS spreads, the Tier 1 ratio and the leverage, appear insignificant in all considered periods, and the liquidity indexes were not important before the crisis.

The studies by Chiaramonte and Casu (2013), Annaert et al. (2013) and Hasan et al. (2015) are those more closely related to our work. However, we differentiate from them for the following reasons. Annaert et al. (2013) limit the sample to European banks; they do not include the ratings in the regression analysis, but they distinguish different sub-samples based on ratings; they do not consider balance-sheet variables as determinants of the CDS spreads but only market variables. Hasan et al. (2015) do not explicitly consider the effects of the ratings. Chiaramonte and Casu (2013) do not consider market and country-level factors nor the ratings. None of these studies consider the sovereign CDS.

## 7.2.2 Studies on CDS and Credit Ratings

The literature focused on CDS and ratings mainly uses event study methodology to test the presence of abnormal movements (in CDS spreads) in the presence of rating changes.

Hull et al. (2004), after examining the relationship between CDS spreads and bond yields, test the relationship between CDS spreads and announcements, reviews and outlooks by rating agencies during the period 1998–2000. Their data set includes over 200,000 CDS spread bids and offers collected by a credit derivatives broker over a 5-year period. They analyse the relationship between the CDS market and rating announcements by carrying two tests. First, they condition on rating events and test whether credit spreads widen before and after rating events. They find that reviews for downgrade contain significant information, but downgrades and negative outlooks do not, and that there is an anticipation of all three types of ratings announcements by the CDS market. Successively, they condition on credit spread changes and test whether the probability of a rating event depends on credit spread level and changes. They find that credit spread changes or credit spread levels provide helpful information in estimating the probability of negative credit rating changes. In the case of positive rating events, the results are much less significant.

Norden and Weber (2004) study the informational efficiency of CDS and stock markets focusing on the impact of credit rating announcements during the period 2000–2002. Their sample includes CDS data provided by a large European bank. They employ event study methodology to test whether these markets respond to rating announcements in terms of abnormal returns and adjusted CDS spread changes. Both stock markets and CDS market demonstrate to be able to anticipate rating downgrades and reviews for downgrade. Furthermore, they show that the magnitude of abnormal returns is affected by the level of the old rating, previous rating events and, only in the CDS market, by the pre-event average rating level.

Di Cesare (2006) studies the ability of market-based indicators (CDS spreads, bond spreads and stock prices) to anticipate rating agencies. He considers a sample of the largest publicly listed international banks from 11 countries during the period 2001–2005. He verifies the presence of "abnormal movements" of the three market indicators before, in concomitance and after rating events (review for rating changes and actual rating changes). He shows that all indicators contain useful information to anticipate rating actions, especially for negative events and that, overall, CDS spreads are relatively more efficient in anticipating negative rating events— stock prices are better predictors in the case of positive rating events.

Burchi and Drago (2012) study the alignment between ratings and CDS focusing on a sample of US firms, in order to demonstrate the existence of a significant difference between the ratings and the CDS that could affect the lending policy of a bank.[4]

# 7.3   Methodology and Data

## 7.3.1  Methodology

We use a framework similar to that used in Annaert et al. (2013) and Hasan et al. (2015). We aim at empirically investigating the determinants of CDS spreads in banks considering three sets of regressors: (i) credit risk variables; (ii) bank-specific variables, including the ratings; and (iii) market and country-level variables, including the sovereign CDS spreads. Since we want to explain and not to predict CDS spreads, we do not lag the explanatory variables.

To test the determinants of CDS spreads in banks, we use the following model:

$$\text{CDS spread}_{it} = \beta_0 + \beta_1 X_{it} + \beta_2 Z_{it} + \beta_3 W_{jt} + \varepsilon_{it}$$

where CDS spread$_{it}$ is the natural log of CDS for bank $i$ at year $t$, $X_{it}$ are the credit risk variables for bank $i$ at year $t$, $Z_{it}$ are the bank-specific variables for bank $i$ at year $t$, $W_{jt}$ are the market and country-level variables for country/geographical area $j$ at year $t$ and $\varepsilon_{it}$ is the idiosyncratic error.

To test whether variables are correlated, we use a Pearson correlation test.[5] We also check and exclude multicollinearity problems by analysing mean Variance inflation factor (VIF) of all the independent variables specified in the linear regression model (mean VIF < 3). In all regression models, we use country-clustered, heteroskedasticity-robust standard errors. We run a pooled OLS regression because the residuals are uncorrelated and OLS standard errors are not biased.[6]

We develop a stepwise analysis. Initially, we use the credit risk variables, and successively we add the bank-specific and the market/country-level variables. Finally, we test a GMM model when the sovereign CDS variable is included. Formally, this model is given by:

$$\text{CDS spread}_{it} = \beta_0 + \beta_1 \text{CDS spread}_{it-1} + \beta_2 X_{it} + \beta_3 Z_{it} + \beta_4 W_{jt} + \varepsilon_{it}$$

We argue that a GMM model is appropriate for several reasons. First, the estimators of Arellano-Bond method (Arellano and Bond 1991) are designed for sample with a small number of time periods (in our sample $T = 4$) and a large number of cross section units ($N = 86$ international banks) that may contain fixed effects and, separate from those fixed effects, idiosyncratic errors that are heteroskedastic and correlated within but not across individuals. Second, sovereign CDS spreads are endogenous to the banks CDS spreads and need to be instrumented accordingly. Third, as the use of the lagged dependent variable introduces autocorrelation in residuals, the dependent variable is instrumented with its lagged value.

## 7.3.2 Data

The empirical analysis focuses on a sample of 86 international banks from 25 countries[7] from 2009 to 2012. Initially, we considered all institutions classified as primary members according to the International Swaps and Derivatives Association (ISDA) guidelines. The initial number of banks was subsequently reduced due to the lack of data on Thomson Reuters Datastream. We ultimately obtained an unbalanced panel, and overall the study analyses 235 bank-year observations. The largest number of banks is from the USA (9), followed by Germany (8) and Italy (7). Even though the sample is geographically heterogeneous, it includes banks that are consistent in terms of transactions on international derivatives markets and all characterised by size and specific requirements to be admitted to ISDA.

Given the limited number of frequencies for some classes of rating and in order to run the regression analysis, we group the sample banks into five classes of ratings (Table 7.1). We can observe a heterogeneity in the distribution of the rating classes, if we consider the presence of five observations on the class B (following the methodology of Standard and Poor's), compared to 188 observations on the class A. The groups belonging to the range from AA+ to AA−(Rating AA) and from A+ to A−(Rating A) are the most consistent in terms of frequency (cumulatively 77.6%) compared to the entire sample.

As dependent variable we use the year-end CDS spreads, a choice strictly related to the type of explanatory variables considered, most with a balance-sheet nature. The data on banks CDS premium is from Thomson Reuters Datastream database over the period from 1 January 2009 to 31 December 2012. Datastream provides comprehensive coverage for firms and banks around the world and it is widely used for research on CDS.

We select the 5-year CDS quotes for senior debt issues since these contracts are generally considered to be the most liquid segments of the market (e.g. Meng and Gwilym 2008) and because they constitute the most important segment of the CDS market. As robustness, starting from the daily CDS spreads, we compute the average of CDS spreads over a year (average year-end CDS spreads) (Hasan et al. 2015).

We are aware that some authors distinguish among different restructuring credit events (and the contractual clauses attached to the restructuring)

Table 7.1 Sample distribution by ratings classes (number of banks in each rating class and the frequency)

| Rating distribution | No of banks | Frequency (%) |
| --- | --- | --- |
| Rating (AA) | 79 | 22.97 |
| Rating (A) | 188 | 54.65 |
| Rating (BBB) | 61 | 17.73 |
| Rating (BB) | 11 | 3.20 |
| Rating (B) | 5 | 1.45 |

Period 2009–2012

(e.g. Hasan et al. 2015). Following other studies (e.g. Chiaramonte and Casu 2013; Annaert et al. 2013; Galil et al. 2014; Pires et al. 2015), in the present work we decide not to consider the different credit events because the data available on Datastream does not always permit to distinguish CDS spreads on the basis of contractual clauses (full, modified, modified, no restructure) and, in fact, many quotations appear as "no value".

Figure 7.1 shows how the CDS premium of sample banks evolved over time. We can observe that the trend is different depending on the rating class. For AA-rated banks the CDS premium increased throughout the period considered. For A-rated and B-rated banks, CDS spreads achieved a peak in 2011 and then decreased in 2012. It seems that A-rated and B-rated banks are more vulnerable to the credit crisis while the AA-rated banks are less subject to the influence of turmoil. This result could be due to the sovereign debt crisis. We observe that CDS spreads of A and B-rated banks decrease with the intensifying of European sovereign debt crisis between 2011 and 2012. It seems that European sovereign debt crisis only affects the AA-rated banks whose CDS spreads continue to increase, while the A and B-rated banks, on average, show a contrary tendency. The composition of our

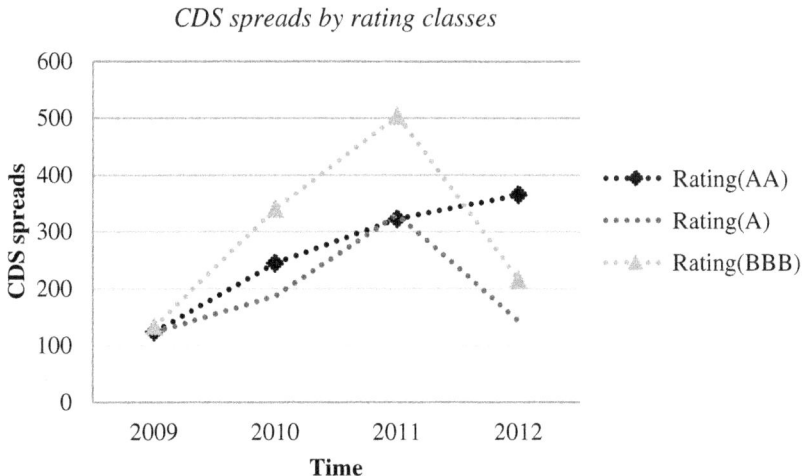

**Fig. 7.1** Time-series plot of the average of year-end CDS spreads by rating classes

sample (the majority of banks is European) might affect the trend of the average CDS spreads between 2011 and 2012.

As independent variables, we consider credit risk factors, bank-specific factors, including the ratings, and market and country-level factors. All data on independent variables are obtained from Datastream. Data on ratings are obtained from Standard and Poor's Global Ratings. The implied volatility indexes data are obtained from different sources.[8]

## 7.4    Variables

### 7.4.1    Credit Risk Variables

Following the literature on credit spreads that relies on Merton's seminal paper (1974), we consider three types of credit risk variable: asset volatility, leverage and risk-free interest rate. Table 7.2 describes the variables and the predicted sign of their coefficients.

*Asset volatility.* Following the previous literature, we consider equity return volatility as a proxy for assets volatility (Ericsson et al. 2009; Annaert et al. 2013; Hasan et al. 2015). Starting from daily stock returns we construct volatility as the historical standard deviation in a particular year. An increase in volatility causes an increase in the default likelihood of the bank. As a consequence, the expected sign of the relationship between asset volatility and the banks CDS spreads is positive.

*Leverage.* Following the previous literature, as leverage measure we use the ratio between the book value of liabilities and the book value of liabilities plus the market value of equity (Galil et al. 2014; Hasan et al. 2015). The level of banks' leverage represents a variable which could positively or negatively influence the level of the CDS premium, depending on the level reached. A small increase in the leverage ratio could have a positive impact because it increases the profitability of a bank and reinforces its capability to repay bondholders and depositors. On the other hand, above a certain threshold, it produces an exponential growth of the risk. As highlighted by Hasan et al. (2015), in the case of banks it is controversial whether higher levels of leverage imply an increase in the bank's credit risk because banks have different asset

**Table 7.2** Description of variables

| Variable | Name | Description | Predicted sign |
|---|---|---|---|
| Credit risk variables | | | |
| Asset volatility | Asset vol | Equity return volatility. The historical standard deviation of bank's daily equity returns in a particular year | + |
| Leverage | Leverage | Book value of liabilities/book value of liabilities + market value of equity. Robustness: Bank stock returns | ± |
| Risk-free rate 5Y | Risk-free rate (5-Y) | Risk-free interest rate. Proxied by the Datastream benchmark 5 year government redemption yield | ± |
| Bank-specific variables | | | |
| Capitalisation | Tier1 | Tier 1 capital ratio. Calculated according to the Basel Accord rules | – |
| Portfolio quality | Asset qual | Provision for loan losses/total loans | + |
| Profitability | ROE | ROE Robustness: Z-score | – |
| Size | Size | Log total assets | ± |
| Liquidity | Liquidity | Net loans/demand deposits | – |
| Market and country-level variables | | | |
| Total return index | TRI | Datastream Total Return Index. The theoretical aggregate growth in value of the constituents of the index | – |
| Market volatility | Mkt vol | Implied volatility index (VIX, VSTOXX, S&P/ASX 200 VIX, HIS volatility index, India VIX, CBOEO EX implied volatility index, VXJ) | + |
| Slope of the yield curve | Slope | Difference between the 10-year and the 5-year treasury bond yields | – |
| GDP | GDP | Log of GDP | + |
| Sovereign CDS | Sov CDS (end) | Sovereign year-end CDS spread | + |

and liability structures from other (non-financial) firms, due to the fact that their leverage ratios are considerably greater than those in other corporate sectors, and there is less variation among banks: the ability to draw on more deposits is a signal of greater growth potential but, at the same time, too much debt (to equity) can lead a bank to failure. In the robustness analysis, we use the bank stock returns as leverage measure (e.g. Annaert et al. 2013). We decided to not use an accounting measure of leverage to avoid the potential problem of multicollinearity when are used in the same regression as explanatory variables leverage and ROE.

*Risk-free interest rate.* We proxy the risk-free interest rate with the 5-year government bond yield using the Datastream benchmark 5-year government redemption yield. This choice appears consistent with the fact that we use the 5-year CDS spread as the dependent variable (Galil et al. 2014; Hasan et al. 2015). The expected relationship between CDS spreads and the risk-free interest is negative. This can be justified by the fact that interest rates are positively related to economic growth that should imply lower default risk. However, as emphasised by Hasan et al. (2015), the relationship could be positive across countries because banks have higher borrowing costs in countries with greater risk-free rates.

## 7.4.2  Bank-Specific Variables

This set of variables includes those suggested by the previous literature and by regulators (Basel Accords and EBA 2015). We use a set of variables aimed at capturing different indicators of the banks' soundness: capitalisation, portfolio quality, profitability, and liquidity. Finally, we control for banks' size.

*Capitalisation.* We consider the Tier 1 ratio as prescribed by Basel Accords (2 and 3) and also by EBA (2015) (that indicates CET1 rather than Tier1 as numerator). Tier 1 ratio represents a global riskiness indicator of the banks.[9] A higher value of this ratio should lower CDS spreads and therefore the expected sign for the coefficient is negative.

Also, the level of leverage (grouped in the credit risk variables) is a bank's capitalisation measure. It is worth noting that the new rules of Basel 3 explicitly include a financial leverage minimum coefficient, constructed as the ratio of Tier 1 capital to total risk exposure (denominator that can be proxied by the total assets). Basel 3 introduces a leverage ratio requirement equal to 3% that is intended to constrain leverage in the banking sector (thus helping to mitigate the risk of the destabilising deleveraging processes which can damage the financial system and the economy) and to introduce additional safeguards against model risk and measurement error by supplementing the risk-based measures (that is Tier 1 ratio and total capital ratio) with a simple, transparent, independent measure of risk.

*Portfolio quality.* Following the previous literature (EBA 2015; Chiaramonte and Casu 2013; Hasan et al. 2015), we expect that asset quality is negatively related to CDS spreads. We consider the provision for loan losses ratio to proxy the asset quality of the banks. A higher ratio indicates that the bank has more bad loans and, therefore, the expected sign of the coefficient is positive.

*Profitability.* Following the previous literature (EBA 2015; Chiaramonte and Casu 2013; Hasan et al. 2015), we use return on equity (ROE), also considered a bank's efficiency indicator. We expect a negative sign of the coefficients of the ROE. Additionally, to take into account the overall banks performance, that is profitability and risk (ECB 2010), in the robustness, we use the Z-score, a measure of riskiness of the bank that combines profitability, leverage, and return volatility in a single indicator, that increases with higher profitability and capitalisation levels, and decreases with unstable earnings (Berger et al. 2009).

*Liquidity.* As a measure of banks' liquidity, we use the net loans/demand deposits ratio.[10] The expected sign of the relationship between liquidity and CDS spreads is negative. The higher the liquidity, the lower should be the probability for banks in incurring in liquidity crisis, the lower should the overall risk of the bank. However, the sign of relationship could be controversial because the liquidity risk has a different nature than the credit risk, that captured by the CDS premium. As the financial crisis demonstrated, the consequences of the liquidity shocks cannot be neglected because, when not adequately managed, they could easily transform the liquidity crisis of the bank in an insolvency problem. The concern about the liquidity risk is confirmed by the attention of regulators towards liquidity and funding position after the financial crisis. Apart from what Basel 3 prescribes in terms of liquidity ratios, this attention is confirmed in Europe by the recent guidelines of European Banking Authority (EBA) about SREP (EBA 2014) where, in order to assess the bank's economic viability, authorities have to review and evaluate the liquidity of the bank, taking into account the liquidity and funding risks.

*Size.* Finally, we control for bank's size proxied by the total assets. The expected sign of the relationship between bank's size and CDS spreads is controversial (De Nicolò 2000; Stever 2007). On one hand, it is expected to be positive because a larger bank may have a greater capacity to absorb risk (Berger et al. 2009). On the other hand, due to the size-related diversification benefits and the economies of scale, the larger banks should be less risky. However, the managers of larger banks could take advantage of the benefits of risk diversification to push the risk profile of the bank further (Hughes et al. 2001). It follows that we have no specific expectations about the sign of this relation.

*Ratings.* Since both ratings and CDS spreads should capture the credit risk of a bank, we expect a positive relationship.

## 7.4.3 Market and Country-Level Variables

Following the previous literature, we consider some market-wide and country-level variables. This empirical strategy is due to several reasons. First, many studies demonstrated that credit risk variables have a limited explanatory power. Second, given the heterogeneity of our sample, that includes banks from very different geographical areas and countries, it seems appropriate to control for these differences. Moreover, banks' performance, risk and regulations are often correlated to economic development (La Porta et al. 1998; Demirgüç-Kunt et al. 2004; Hasan et al. 2015). Third, as several studies have shown, default probabilities and recovery rates are influenced by the business cycle (e.g. Altman et al. 2005). Fourth, the importance of macroeconomic factors in assessing the risk of a bank is recognised by regulators (EBA 2015). As a consequence, in our empirical analysis we consider some market-wide indicators (total return index, market volatility, slope of the term structure) and some country-level indicators (GDP and sovereign CDS spreads).

*The total return index*. Following the previous literature (e.g., Annaert et al. 2013), we include a market-wide stock index return as control variable. We use Datastream Total Return Index with reference to the region of the world in which the company is domiciled.[11] When the general business climate improves, the defaults probabilities should decrease (an increase in recovery rates is also expected). Therefore, the expected relationship with CDS spreads is negative.

*Market volatility*. Following the previous literature (Collin-Dufresne et al. 2001; Annaert et al. 2013; Galil et al. 2014), we include the implied volatility indexes as control variable. We use different indexes taking into account the region of the world in which the company is listed. Given the heterogeneity of some countries which are located on the same geographic area, in some cases, when available, we use country-specific implied volatility indexes. Specifically, we use VIX for the USA, VSTOXX for Europe, S&P/ASX 200 VIX for Australia, HIS volatility index for China, India VIX for India, CBOEO EX implied volatility index for emerging markets, VXJ for Japan. A higher volatility implies a higher economic uncertainty, an increase in investors' risk aversion (Annaert et al. 2013) and, therefore, a higher risk. As a consequence, a positive relationship with the CDS premium is expected.

*Slope of the term structure*. Following the previous literature (Ericsson et al. 2009; Annaert et al. 2013; Galil et al. 2014), we include the slope of the term structure as control variable, defined as the difference between the 10-year and the 2-year treasury bond yields obtained from Datastream of the benchmark series. Also, the slope of the term structure is considered an important signal of the future business cycle. A higher slope predicts an improvement in business cycle and indicates that interest rates tend to increase. Both arguments should be related to a decrease in credit risk and, therefore, a negative sign of the coefficient is predicted.

*GDP*. We control for GDP of each country in which the sample bank is listed. An expected positive relationship with CDS spreads is expected.

*Sovereign CDS spreads*. The previous literature did not explicitly consider this variable. However, given the special nature of the companies included in our sample and taking into account that banks typically own a significant volume of sovereign bonds in their portfolio,[12] we decided to include this variable. Taking into account the very special period of analysis that we are interested in, during which several countries experienced a sovereign debt crisis, this choice seems appropriate. The importance of sovereign CDS spreads in assessing the risk of a bank is also recognised by regulators. For instance, in its recent guidelines on the minimum list of qualitative and quantitative recovery plan indicators, EBA (2015) explicitly includes the sovereign CDS. We are aware of the possible analysis limitations arising from the potential endogeneity between banks' CDS and sovereign risk (captured by sovereign CDS). To solve this problem, when the sovereign CDS variable is included in the regression model we use a GMM model. Notwithstanding this econometric strategy, we argue that the results of the estimates should be discussed with caution given the very complex and debated relationship between bank and sovereign risk.

## 7.4.4  Descriptive Statistics

Table 7.3 outlines the descriptive statistics of independent and dependent variables. The mean of year-end CDS spreads is 235.48 basis points with a standard deviation of 32.188 basis points. The mean of average year-end CDS spreads is 233.04 with a standard deviation of 25.526. Both CDS spreads record very similar mean values. However, the lower standard deviation of the average year-end CDS spreads, due to the construction of this variable, implies that the average year-end CDS spread is more stable than the year-end CDS spread. The year-end CDS spreads range from 100 to 2646.39 basis points whereas the average year-end CDS range from 100 to 1955.43 basis points.

Panel A describes the variables divided into three groups: credit risk variables, bank-specific variables and market and country-level variables.

Panel B reports the summary statistics of CDS spreads based on the rating classes. It is interesting to note that the ratings and CDS spreads are not always aligned. This is observable both when we take into account the mean values and when we consider the maximum values. In particular, A-rated banks show a CDS average spread less than that

**Table 7.3** Summary statistics of full sample and divided by rating classes

| Variables | No of obs | Mean | STD | Min | Max | Units |
|---|---|---|---|---|---|---|
| **Dependent variable** | | | | | | |
| Year-end CDS | 235 | 235.48 | 32.188 | 100.00 | 2646.39 | Basis points |
| Average year-end CDS | 235 | 233.04 | 25.526 | 100.00 | 1955.43 | Basis points |
| **Panel A: Independent variables** | | | | | | |
| *Credit risk variables* | | | | | | |
| Asset vol | 235 | 2.44 | 1.669 | 0.00 | 10.21 | % |
| Leverage | 235 | 89.74 | 0.051 | 78.13 | 98.96 | % |
| Risk-free rate (5Y) | 235 | 2.77 | 1.162 | 0.49 | 7.23 | % |
| *Bank-specific variables* | | | | | | |
| Tier1 | 235 | 11.24 | 6.177 | 0.01 | 23.27 | % |
| Asset qual | 235 | 1.03 | 1.073 | 0.00 | 7.62 | % |
| ROE | 235 | 8.69 | 8.765 | 0.00 | 50.93 | % |
| Z-score | 235 | 7.32 | 10.508 | 0.14 | 75.64 | % |
| Size | 235 | 19.82 | 1.216 | 16.98 | 21.80 | Logs |
| Liquidity | 235 | 5.98 | 7.292 | 0.46 | 44.31 | % |
| *Market and country-level variables* | | | | | | |
| TRI | 235 | 8.30 | 0.904 | 3.83 | 8.95 | Logs |
| Mkt vol | 235 | 23.21 | 4.605 | 14.70 | 32.15 | % |
| Slope | 235 | 1.49 | 0.56 | 0.51 | 3.55 | % |
| GDP | 235 | 12.75 | 2.276 | 7.81 | 18.58 | Logs |
| Sov CDS (end) | 235 | 262.36 | 1389.61 | 10.79 | 14909.36 | Basis points |
| **Panel B: CDS spreads by rating classes** | | | | | | |
| Rating (AA) | | | | | | |
| Year-end CDS | 57 | 251.11 | 326.66 | 1.00 | 1490.38 | Basis points |
| Average year-end CDS | 57 | 255.17 | 313.53 | 1.00 | 1955.43 | Basis points |
| Rating (A) | | | | | | |
| Year-end CDS | 137 | 187.78 | 235.427 | 38.00 | 2646.39 | Basis points |
| Average year-end CDS | 137 | 189.93 | 147.929 | 47.04 | 1572.27 | Basis points |
| Rating (BBB) | | | | | | |
| Year end CDS | 33 | 324.34 | 343.844 | 47.23 | 1941.50 | Basis points |
| Average year-end CDS | 33 | 326.16 | 269.226 | 50.00 | 1199.07 | Basis points |
| Rating (BB) | | | | | | |
| Year-end CDS | 7 | 917.99 | 800.255 | 108.47 | 2576.55 | Basis points |
| Average year-end CDS | 7 | 806.58 | 597.334 | 192.32 | 1938.56 | Basis points |
| Rating (B) | | | | | | |
| Year-end CDS | 1 | 446.04 | 186.100 | 81.94 | 446.04 | Basis points |
| Average year-end CDS | 1 | 601.69 | 263.722 | 133.57 | 601.69 | Basis points |

of AA-rated banks. This evidence is in contrast with the fact that ratings and CDS spreads are both aimed at capturing the same phenomenon (the credit risk). As evidenced by Burchi and Drago (2012), while the misalignment between ratings and market credit spreads is known in the literature, the reasons that explain the valuation differences are still relatively little explored. In recent years, a number of studies suggest that these differences are due to a different assessment of certain systematic risk and market-wide factors, such as liquidity (Perraudin and Taylor 2004; Becker and Ivashina 2015; Elton et al. 2001), not reflected by the ratings and, instead, captured by CDS spreads.

## 7.5    Results

In this section, we study the explanatory power of the different factors considered in our model. As dependent variable we consider CDS spreads at the end of each year. We develop a stepwise analysis (Table 7.4).

Initially, we estimate the coefficients of the credit risk variables (column 1, Model I). Successively, we add the bank-specific variables (column 2, Model II) and the rating (column 3, Model III). Afterwards, we test the model by also using the market/country-level variables (column 4, Model IV). Finally, we add the sovereign CDS variable (column 5, GMM Model).

When only the credit risk variables are considered, the results show that none of the regressors is statistically significant. This result is not surprising given the very special sector and period that we consider. As emphasised by the previous literature (e.g. Hasan et al. 2015), the credit spread puzzle is more pronounced in the case of banks. Furthermore, as demonstrated by previous studies, the determinants of the CDS spread vary across time (Annaert et al. 2013), and this effect could be more pronounced during a crisis period (financial crisis and sovereign debt crisis). These preliminary findings indicate that other factors have to be considered to explain the CDS spreads.

When also the bank-specific variables are considered, the explanatory power of the model increases. Model II and III present an adjusted

**Table 7.4**  Results of OLS regression.

| Dependent variable: year-end CDS spreads | | | | | |
|---|---|---|---|---|---|
| log (CDS end) | Model I | Model II | Model III | Model IV | GMM |
| $log(CDSend)_{t-1}$ | | | | | 0.4735** |
| | | | | | (0.202) |
| Asset vol | −0.0996 | −0.1453 | 0.1810* | 0.2267** | 0.6702** |
| | (0.078) | (0.107) | (0.101) | (0.089) | (0.299) |
| Leverage | −0.3912 | −0.2813 | −0.4931 | 0.6319 | 0.6498 |
| | (0.628) | (0.919) | (0.962) | (0.833) | (0.718) |
| Risk-free rate (5Y) | 0.1396 | 0.0426 | 0.0600 | −0.0319 | 0.0902 |
| | (0.088) | (0.053) | (0.059) | (0.056) | (0.091) |
| Tier1 | | −0.0777*** | −0.0817*** | −0.0918*** | −0.1366** |
| | | (0.013) | (0.014) | (0.022) | (0.067) |
| Asset qual | | 0.1364 | 0.0392 | 0.1791** | 0.1068* |
| | | (0.096) | (0.078) | (0.089) | (0.062) |
| ROE | | 0.0124 | 0.0199 | 0.0162 | −0.0065 |
| | | (0.011) | (0.015) | (0.012) | (0.025) |
| Size | | −0.2573*** | -0.3050** | −0.2092** | −0.1301*** |
| | | (0.094) | (0.124) | (0.105) | (0.029) |
| Liquidity | | −0.0121** | −0.0094 | 0.0001 | 0.0069 |
| | | (0.005) | (0.006) | (0.008) | (0.034) |
| Rating (AA) | | | | | |
| Rating (A) | | | 0.0751 | −0.0928 | 1.7143* |
| | | | (0.156) | (0.154) | (0.974) |
| Rating (BBB) | | | 0.3071 | 0.2558 | 0.3267 |
| | | | (0.356) | (0.328) | (0.240) |
| Rating (BB) | | | 1.2751*** | 0.8533** | 0.8940*** |
| | | | (0.372) | (0.336) | (0.309) |
| Rating (B) | | | 0.4854 | 0.4212 | 1.1707 |
| | | | (0.582) | (0.537) | (1.766) |
| TRI | | | | −0.0460 | 0.6568 |
| | | | | (0.124) | (0.425) |
| Mkt vol | | | | 0.0625*** | 0.0962** |
| | | | | (0.013) | (0.047) |
| Slope | | | | −0.1924** | -0.1264** |
| | | | | (0.077) | (0.062) |
| GDP | | | | 0.0482 | 0.1971 |
| | | | | (0.056) | (0.152) |
| Sov CDS (end) | | | | | 0.3507*** |
| | | | | | (0.038) |

(continued)

Table 7.4  (continued)

| Dependent variable: year-end CDS spreads | | | | | |
|---|---|---|---|---|---|
| log (CDS end) | Model I | Model II | Model III | Model IV | GMM |
| $log(CDSend)_{t-1}$ | | | | | 0.4735** |
| Constant | 5.2534*** | 7.9008*** | 6.5640*** | 5.6725** | −16.0593** |
| | (0.619) | (1.550) | (2.299) | (2.300) | (6.915) |
| No. of observations | 235 | 235 | 235 | 235 | 235 |
| $R^2$ | 0.0439 | 0.1415 | 0.2157 | 0.3485 | |
| Country clustering | Y | Y | Y | Y | |
| VIF[1] | 1.02 | 1.3 | 1.58 | 1.74 | |
| Sargan test | | | | | 0.006 |
| Hansen test | | | | | 0.004 |

The dependent variable is the natural logarithm of the year-end CDS spreads
Period 2009–2012
This table reports the results of OLS regression. Robust standard errors (clustered at the country level) are in parenthesis below the estimated coefficients. ***, ** and * indicate statistical significance at the 1–5% and 10% level, respectively. VIF is the variation inflation factor;[1] mean VIF values greater than 10 may warrant further examination
Asset volatility (Asset vol) is the historical standard deviation of bank's daily equity returns in a particular year. Leverage is the ratio between book value of liabilities and the sum of book value of liabilities and market value of equity . The risk-free interest rate with 5-year maturity (Risk-free rate (5-Y)) is proxied by the Datastream benchmark 5-year government redemption yield. Tier 1 ratio (Tier1) ratio is calculated according to the Basel Accord rules. Asset quality (Asset qual) is the ratio between provision for loan losses and total loans. ROE is return on assets. Size is the natural logarithm of total asset. Liquidity is the ratio between net loans and demand deposits. Total return index (TRI) is the theoretical aggregate growth in value of the constituents of the index. Market volatility (Mkt vol) is the implied volatility index. Slope of the yield curve (Slope) is the difference between the 10-year and the 5-year treasury bond yields. GDP is natural logarithm of GDP of each country. Sovereign CDS spreads (Sov CDS (end)) are the sovereign CDS spreads of each country. Rating AA is the reference rating of our regression

R–squared of 14.15 and 21.57%, respectively. In Model II we use the bank-specific variables while in Model III we also consider the rating. It seems that Model III is better able to capture the determinants of CDS spreads. If we focus on the bank-specific variables, results reported in column 2 show that banks' capitalisation (measured by the Tier 1 capital ratio) has a significant explanatory power with the expected negative sign. This result is confirmed by all the estimates that we run in the present work. We argue that one of the main indicators that market participants consider when assessing the banks' risk is the level of capitalisation. This result is in line with the previous studies (Chiaramonte and Casu 2013; Hasan et al. 2015) and also with the regulators indications that consider the capital buffers as the most important defence against the potential bankruptcy. Capitalisation is important also to protect deposits and to survive during a crisis or to external shocks. This result confirms that markets and regulators are aligned when assessing the banks' risk.

The banks' liquidity proves to be significant with the expected negative sign (Kanagaretnam et al. 2016) only in Model II while it loses its importance in the other estimates. This can be due to the fact that liquidity risk and credit risk (captured by CDS spreads) have a different nature. Findings on the importance of liquidity in determining the banks' (credit) risk are only partially consistent with concerns and expectations of regulators (EBA 2015) that, especially after the turmoil, started to consider liquidity as an important source of risk.

The size variable presents a significant coefficient (at 1%) with negative sign, signalling that larger banks are perceived by the market participants as less risky. As emphasised in previous sections, the relationship between bank's size and CDS spreads is controversial. In our case, the negative effect of the size can be due to the potential ability of larger banks to achieve diversification benefits and economies of scale. Furthermore, this result seems to confirm the too-big-to-fail paradigm since larger banks are perceived as less risky. Also this result is confirmed by all the estimates carried out in the present work.

In Model III, we test the model including the credit risk variables and the bank-specific variables, plus the ratings. The results confirm the significance of capitalisation and size and show that ratings affect the CDS premium. The ratings variables are significant when we pass from investment to non-investment grade banks. The coefficient of the rating BB variable is strongly significant (at 1%) and the sign of the coefficient is positive. For the interpretation of the sign of the coefficient, we have to consider that the control group in our estimates is the AA-rating group of banks. The sign and the values of the coefficients of the rating classes are consistent with our expectations. When the rating decreases, the CDS premium increases and this increase is significant when switching from investment to non-investment grade banks. This result is always confirmed.

In Model IV, we test the complete model, adding the market and country-level variables. As expected, the explanatory power of the model increases (adjusted R–squared equal to 34.85%). Overall, findings show that market and country-level variables are important in explaining CDS spreads. With reference to the credit risk and the bank-specific variables, these findings substantially confirm the results previously obtained. When the market and country-level variables are included, the asset volatility tends to gain significance with the expected positive sign. Also, the asset quality variable is significant at 5% with the expected positive sign. A higher ratio of bad loans positively affects the bank's credit risk. This result is consistent with the previous literature (Chiaramonte and Casu 2013; Hasan et al. 2015; Kanagaretnam et al. 2016) and indicates that market participants and regulators tend to be aligned (EBA 2015). Since the most important assets of the banks' portfolio are represented by loans, this result highlights the CDS capacity to capture the credit risk of a bank. Among market and country-level factors, the variables market volatility and slope of the yield curve are significant (at 1 and 5%, respectively) with the expected sign of the coefficients. Findings indicate that, in the case of banks, the market variables affect their credit risk. However, this conclusion has to be contextualised taking into account the specialness of the period considered; in fact, the years from 2009 to 2012 were characterised by the crisis in many countries and geographical area, such as Europe.

The findings obtained so far seem to indicate the importance of market and country-level factors in determining the banks' CDS spread. Because since 2011 some countries have experienced the sovereign debt crisis, we decided to further investigate this issue by explicitly considering the sovereign CDS spread as determinants of the banks CDS spread. In column 5, we report the results of the estimates obtained using the GMM model. The findings demonstrate that sovereign CDS spreads strongly affect the banks' CDS while the results of the other variables tend to be stable in term of significance with respect to those obtained from previous estimates. The results of the sovereign CDS variable are probably due to the high percentage of sovereign bonds present in the asset portfolios of the most important international banks. However, as previously emphasised, these results should be considered

**Table 7.5** Results of the normalised beta of the OLS regression

| Normalised beta | | | | |
|---|---|---|---|---|
| | Model I | Model II | Model III | Model IV |
| Asset vol | −0.1237 | −0.1863 | 0.2320 | 0.2963 |
| Leverage | −0.0506 | −0.0386 | −0.0677 | 0.0873 |
| Risk-free rate (5Y) | 0.1838 | 0.0598 | 0.0841 | −0.0462 |
| Tier1 | | −0.0559 | −0.0588 | −0.1237 |
| Asset qual | | 0.1328 | 0.0382 | 0.1787 |
| ROE | | 0.2643 | 0.2231 | 0.1841 |
| Size | | −0.1932 | −0.0764 | −0.1390 |
| Liquidity | | −0.1206 | −0.0944 | 0.0012 |
| Rating (AA) | | | | |
| Rating (A) | | | 0.0466 | −0.0576 |
| Rating (BBB) | | | 0.1447 | 0.1084 |
| Rating (BB) | | | 0.3165 | 0.2189 |
| Rating (B) | | | 0.0501 | 0.0449 |
| TRI | | | | −0.0422 |
| Mkt vol | | | | 0.3638 |
| Slope | | | | −0.1654 |
| GDP | | | | 0.1143 |

The dependent variable is the natural logarithm of the year-end CDS spreads
Period 2009–2012
This table reports the results of the normalised beta of the OLS regressions
Asset volatility (Asset vol) is the historical standard deviation of bank's daily equity returns in a particular year. Leverage is the ratio between book value of liabilities and the sum of book value of liabilities and market value of equity. The risk-free interest rate with 5-year maturity (Risk-free rate (5-Y)) is prox-ied by the Datastream benchmark 5-year government redemption yield. Tier 1 ratio (Tier1) ratio is calculated according to the Basel Accord rules. Asset qual-ity (Asset qual) is the ratio between provision for loan losses and total loans. ROE is return on assets. Size is the natural logarithm of total asset. Liquidity is the ratio between net loans and demand deposits. Total return index (TRI) is the theoretical aggregate growth in value of the constituents of the index. Market volatility (Mkt vol) is the implied volatility index. Slope of the yield curve (Slope) is the difference between the 10-year and the 5-year treasury bond yields. GDP is natural logarithm of GDP of each country. Rating AA is the reference rating of our regression

with caution given the very complex and debated relationship between bank and sovereign risk.

The coefficients in Table 7.4 can be misleading if one omits the standard deviations from the analysis. In Table 7.5 we report the nor-malised betas of the regressions that allow us to compare the impact of the independent variables on the banks' CDS spreads. If we focus on the complete model (column 4, Model IV of Table 7.4), we can observe that the variable that has the greatest effect on the CDS spread is the market volatility. A one standard deviation increase in market volatility from its trend is associated with an increase of more than 1/3 of a standard deviation of CDS spreads relative to its own trend. It is worth to note that also Tier 1, asset volatility, asset quality, size and BB rating variables have a strong impact on the CDS spreads of banks.

## 7.6   Robustness Tests

In this section, to further verify our results, we implement some robustness checks concerning the model specification and the estimation method.[13]

First, we use an alternative measure of CDS spreads to check whether our results are sensitive to our choice of the year-end CDS spreads. As dependent variable, we use the average of year-end CDS spreads. The results are qualitatively similar to those obtained previously and reported in Table 7.4.

Our main results are confirmed by this robustness test: (i) by adding the bank-specific and the market/country variables to the model, its explanatory power tends to increase; (ii) when the bank-specific variables are considered, their relative importance in determining CDS spreads is higher than the importance of the credit risk variables; (iii) the BB-rating variable is always strongly significant; (iv) when the market and country-level variables are included, almost all the variables aimed at capturing the general business climate prove to be significant.

Second, given the importance that leverage typically assumes in explaining CDS spreads, we perform tests by using another measure of leverage. As suggested by the previous literature, we employ the bank stock returns (Annaert et al. 2013). The results confirm the previous findings with the leverage variable not showing statistical significance. This indicates that CDS spreads are not sensitive to the definition of leverage.

Third, given the insignificance of the ROE, we use an alternative measure of the profitability of the bank. We perform a test employing the Z-score that does not prove to be significant and therefore confirming previous results.

Finally, we re-estimate all regressions by using a Panel data model with bank fixed effects to account for unobserved time-invariant bank characteristics.[14] The findings generally confirm our main results reported in Table 7.4.

## 7.7 Conclusions

This study examines the determinants of CDS spreads in banks during 2009–2012. Consistent with the previous literature, empirical findings generally show that banks-specific and market and country-level variables affect CDS spreads. One of the main indicators that market participants consider when assessing the banks' risk is the level of capitalisation; this result is in line with regulators indications that consider the capital buffers as the most important defence against the potential bankruptcy. Also the size of the bank proves to be a significant determinant of the CDS spreads, signalling that larger banks are perceived by the market participants as less risky. The ratings of the banks are significant when switching from investment to non-investment grade banks. The sovereign CDS spreads affect the banks' CDS.

Our findings demonstrate that market participants attribute great importance to market and country factors. A hypothesis that can explain these results relates to the period under investigation during which the banks have been affected by the financial turmoil and the sovereign debt crisis in several European countries. It is plausible to expect that when there is no financial panic and a lower level of speculative activity, therefore when markets tend to be more stable, the importance of each of the possible determinants of CDS spreads changes. Given the changed scenario—with the crisis that have been overcome, at least in some countries—, given the new rules in several banking sectors (Basel 3, European Banking Union, and so on), and given the sovereign debt relief, future research could focus on the issues investigated in the present work to study whether and how the determinants of banks CDS spreads vary across time.

Our findings could provide insight for regulators. Results of the empirical analysis could indicate that CDS could function as a catalyst, increasing the speed with which a crisis may spread. This insight is confirmed by the importance of sovereign CDS as determinant of the bank's CDS spreads. Since banks have demonstrated to be transmitters of financial stress, with dangerous effects on the financial stability, regulators should pay more specific attention to the CDS market in banking systems, also to mitigate the procyclical effect frightened by critics of the Basel Accords. Furthermore, our findings corroborate the efforts made by policy makers in increasing the requirements and transparency of credit rating agencies and in searching new strategies to face the too-big-to-fail paradigm. Finally, the results seem to indicate that regulators and market participants are aligned when considering the importance of capitalisation in determining the banks' risk.

# Notes

1. See "Bank Recovery and Resolution Directive" n. 2014/59/EU.
2. Another problem highlighted by empirical studies is related to the fact that the impact of structural default factors is time-varying.
3. The acronym CAMELS is derived from the components of a bank's condition that supervisors assess using a mix of publicly available and private information to assign a composite overall rating. These components are as follows: C (Capital Adequacy), A (Asset Quality), M (Management), E (Earnings), L (Liquidity) and S (Sensitivity to Market Risk).
4. Drago and Gallo (2016) study the relationship between ratings announcement and CDS premium with reference to sovereign. Using event study methodology, they test the impact of rating changes announcements (given by Standard & Poor's) on the euro-area sovereign CDS market during the period 2004–2013. They show that when downgrades are considered, there is a significant effect on the CDS market, especially for speculative grade countries. When upgrades are considered they demonstrate the existence of a more limited impact: only on the announcement day and on the following day. Furthermore, they find that outlooks are not significant while negative reviews have an impact only on the days following the announcement.

5. Pearson correlation matrix does not show problems of correlation among independent variables because all correlation coefficients are lower than 50%. Additionally, the correlation coefficients between CDS spreads and each of the independent variables have the expected sign. Asset quality, ROE, slope of the yield curve and market volatility are the variables with the strongest and statistically significant correlation with CDS spreads. For the sake of brevity, we decide to not show the correlation matrix, available upon request.

6. We test the autocorrelation of the error term by using a Durbin–Watson statistics. In all regressions, the observed statistics is greater than the upper value in Durbin–Watson table. Therefore, we do not reject the null hypothesis of non-autocorrelated errors.

7. The countries are as follows: Abu Dhabi, Australia, Austria, Belgium, China, Denmark, France, Germany, Japan, Greece, India, Ireland, Italy, Malaysia, Norway, the Netherlands, Portugal, Singapore, South Korea, Spain, Sweden, Switzerland, Turkey, the UK, the USA.

8. VSTOXX data are obtained from The Wall Street Journal (www.wsj.com); VIX data from CBOE (www.cboe.com); S&P/ASX 200 VIX and HIS volatility index from www.investing.com; India VIX from the National Stock Exchange of India (www.nseindia.com); CBOEO EX implied volatility index from https://sg.finance.yahoo.com; VXJ Japan from the Center for Mathematical Modeling and Data Science (Osaka University) (www-mmds.sigmath.es.osaka-u.ac.jp/en/).

9. Some authors emphasised that Tier 1 ratio suffers several limitations such as the calculation of risk-weighted assets (RWA) (Vallascas and Hagendorff 2013), the different definitions across jurisdictions and the lack of information to enable operators to fully evaluate and compare the quality of capital among institutions (BIS 2011).

10. The lower the loans, the greater the reserves of the front line that banks can use to bridge the liquidity imbalances (government bonds).

11. Given their specialness and given the data availability, for China and India we employed the country total return index. The return index represents the theoretical aggregate growth in value of the constituents of the index. The index constituents are deemed to return an aggregate daily dividend which is included as an incremental amount to the daily change in price index.

12. The economic policies of the European Central Bank (long-term refinancing operation, LTRO, and quantitative easing) have recently

allowed banks to buy many government bonds and take advantage of the carry trade mechanism.

13. For the sake of brevity, we decide to not show the results, available upon request.

14. We estimate the Panel data with random and fixed effects. The Hausman test indicates that fixed effect is more appropriate.

# References

Aktung, E. G., Vasconcellos, and Y. Bae. 2009. The dynamics of sovereign credit default swap and bond markets: Empirical evidence from the 2001–2007 period. *Applied Economics Letters* 19: 251–259.

Altman, E.I., B. Brady, A. Resti, and A. Sironi. 2005. The link between default and recovery rates: Theory, empirical evidence and implications. *Journal of Business* 78: 2203–2227.

Amato, J.D., and E.M. Remolona. 2003. The credit spread puzzle. *BIS Quarterly Review*, December, 51–63.

Ammer, J., and F. Cai. 2011. Sovereign CDS and bond pricing dynamics in emerging markets: Does the cheapest-to-deliver option matter? *Journal of International Financial Markets, Institutions and Money* 21 (3): 369–387.

Annaert, J., M. De Ceuster, P. Van Roy, and C. Vespro. 2013. What determines Euro area bank CDS spreads? *Journal of International Money and Finance* 32: 444–461.

Arellano, M., and S. Bond. 1991. Some tests of specification for panel data: Monte Carlo evidence and an application to employment equations. *The Review of Economic Studies*, 277–297.

Augustin, P., M.G. Subrahmanyam, D.Y. Tang, and S.Q. Wang. 2014. Credit default swaps: A survey. *Foundations and Trends in Finance* 9 (1–2): 1–196.

Becker, B., and V. Ivashina. 2015. Reaching for yield in the bond market. *Journal of Finance* 5: 1863–1901.

Berger, A.N., L.F. Klapper, and R.-Ariss Turk. Bank competition and financial stability. *Journal of Financial Services Research* 35 (2): 99–118.

BIS. 2011. Basilea 3—Schema di regolamentazione internazionale per il rafforzamento delle banche e dei sistemi bancari. *Basel Committee.*

Blanco, R., S. Brennan, and I. Marsh. 2005. An empirical analysis of the dynamic relationship between investment-grade bonds and credit default swaps. *Journal of Finance* 60: 2255–2281.

Boss, M., and M. Scheicher. 2005. The determinants of credit spread changes in the Euro area. *Bank for International Settlements.*

Burchi, A., and D. Drago. 2012. Are credit ratings and CDS spreads aligned? The implications for regulation and loan pricing. *Bancaria* 10: 42–65.

Carboni, A. 2011. The sovereign credit default swap market: Price discovery, volumes and links with banks' risk premia. Bank of Italy Temi di Discussione Working paper 821.

Chiaramonte, L., and B. Casu. 2013. The determinants of bank CDS spreads: Evidence from the financial crisis. *European Journal of Finance* 19: 861–887.

Collin-Dufresne, P., R.S. Goldstein, and J.S. Martin. 2001. The determinants of credit spread changes. *Journal of Finance* 56 (6): 2177–2207.

Coudert, V., and M. Gex. 2010. Credit default swap and bond markets: Which leads the other? *Financial Stability Review, Banque de France* 14: 161–167.

De Nicolò G. 2000. Size, charter value and risk in banking: an international perspective. International Finance Discussion Paper 689, Board of Governors of the Federal Reserve System, Washington, DC.

Demirguc-Kunt, A., L. Laeven, and R. Levine. 2004. Regulations, market structure, institutions, and the cost of financial intermediation. *Journal Money Credit Bank* 36: 593–622.

Di Cesare A. 2006. Do market-based indicators anticipate rating agencies? Evidence for international banks. Bank of Italy Temi di Discussione Working Paper 593: 1–42.

Di Cesare A., and G. Guazzarotti. 2010. An analysis of the determinants of credit default swap spread changes before and during the subprime financial turmoil. Bank of Italy Temi di Discussione Working Paper 749.

Drago, D., and R. Gallo. 2016. The impact and the spillover effect of a sovereign rating announcement on the Euro area CDS market. *Journal of International Money and Finance* 67: 264–286.

Driessen, J. 2005. Is default event risk priced in corporate bonds? *Review of Financial Studies* 18 (1): 165–195.

Düllmann, K., and A. Sosinska. 2007. Credit default swap prices as risk indicators of listed German banks. *Financial Markets and Portfolio Management* 21: 269–292.

EBA. 2014. Guidelines on common procedures and methodologies for the supervisory review and evaluation process (SREP), 19 December: 1–218.

EBA. 2015. Guidelines on the minimum list of qualitative and quantitative recovery plan indicators. Final Report 6 May: 1–41.

ECB. 2010. Beyond ROE–How to measure bank performance. *European Central Bank.*

Elton, E.J., M.J. Gruber, D. Agrawal, and C. Mann. 2001. Explaining the rate spread on corporate bonds. *Journal of Finance* 56 (1): 247–277.

Ericsson, J., K. Jacobs, and R. Oviedo. 2009. The determinants of credit default swap premia. *Journal of Financial and Quantitative Analysis* 44 (1): 109–132.

European Commission. 2014. Quarterly Report on the Euro Area 13 (4): 1–38.

FitchRatings. 2007. Fitch CDS implied ratings Model, 13 June.

Fontana, A., and M. Scheicher. 2010. An analysis of Euro area sovereign CDS and their relation with government bonds. *European Central Bank* Working papers, *1271*, December: 1–47.

Galil, K., O.M. Shapir, D. Amiram, and U. Ben-Zion. 2014. The determinants of CDS spreads. *Journal of Banking & Finance* 41: 271–282.

Hasan, I., L. Liu, and G. Zhang. 2015. The determinants of global bank credit-default-swap spreads. *Journal of Financial Services Research*: 1–45.

Heinz, F.F., and Y. Sun. 2014. Sovereign CDS Spreads in Europe—The role of global risk aversion, economic fundamentals, liquidity, and spillovers. *IMF* Working paper, WP/14/17.

Hughes, J.P., L.J. Mester, and C. Moon. 2001. Are scale economies in banking elusive or illusive? Evidence obtained by incorporating capital structure and risk-taking into models of bank production checking accounts and bank monitoring, *Journal of Banking.*

Hull, J., M. Predescu, and A. White. 2004. The Relationship between credit default swap spreads, bond yields, and credit rating announcements. *Journal of Banking & Finance* 28 (11): 2789–2811.

IMF. 2013. A new look at the role of sovereign credit default swap. *Global Financial Stability Report*, April: Chapter 2, 57–92.

Kanagaretnam, K., G. Zhang, and S.B. Zhang. 2016. CDS pricing and accounting disclosures: Evidence from US bank holding corporations around the recent financial crisis. *Journal of Financial Stability* 22: 33–44.

La Porta, R., F. Lopez-de-Silanes, A. Shleifer, and R. Vishny. 1998. Law and finance. *Journal of Political Economy* 106 (6): 1113–1155.

Liu, L., G. Zhang, and Y. Fang. 2016. Bank credit default swaps and deposit insurance around the world. *Journal of International Money and Finance.*

Meng, L., and O.A. Gwilym. 2008. The determinants of CDS bid-ask spreads. *Journal of Derivatives*: 70–80.

Merton, R.C. 1974. On the pricing of corporate debt: The risk structure of interest rates. *Journal of Finance* 29 (2): 449–470.

Minton, B.A., R. Stulz, and R. Williamson. 2009. How much do banks use credit derivatives to hedge loans? *Journal of Financial Service Research* 35 (1): 1–31.

Norden, L., and M. Weber. 2004. Informational efficiency of credit default swap and stock markets: The impact of credit rating announcements. *Journal of Banking & Finance* 28: 2813–2843.

O'Kane, D., and S. Sen. 2005. Credit spreads explained. *Journal of Credit Risk* 1: 61–78.

Perraudin, W., and A.P. Taylor. 2004. On the consistency of ratings and bond market yields. *Journal of Banking & Finance* 28: 2769–2788.

Pires, P., J.P. Pereira, and L.F. Martins. 2015. The empirical determinants of credit default swap spreads: A quantile regression approach. *European Financial Management* 21 (3): 556–589.

Raunig, B., and M. Scheicher. 2009. Are banks different? Evidence from the CDS Market. Oesterreichische National Bank Working paper 152: 1–39.

Stever, R. 2007. Bank size, credit and the sources of bank market risk. *BIS* Working paper 238: 1–31.

Vallascas, F., and J. Hagendorff. 2013. The risk sensitivity of capital requirements: Evidence from an international sample of large banks. *Review of Finance* 17 (6): 1947–1988.

Zhang, B.Y., H. Zhou, and H. Zhu. 2009. Explaining credit default swap spreads with equity volatility and jump risks of individual firms. *Review of Financial Studies* 22 (12): 5099–5131.

# Index

Printed by Printforce, the Netherlands